My Family History

My Life in Charleston

Lavern Lincoln

authorHOUSE®

AuthorHouse™
1663 Liberty Drive
Bloomington, IN 47403
www.authorhouse.com
Phone: 1 (800) 839-8640

Published by AuthorHouse 11/02/2017

ISBN: 978-1-5246-9294-0 (sc)
ISBN: 978-1-5246-9293-3 (e)

Print information available on the last page.

CONTENTS

Acknowledgement vii

Chapter 1   Early Childhood and Family Background 1

Chapter 2   Teenage Years 51

Chapter 3   Adulthood 59

Chapter 4   Overview 100

ACKNOWLEDGEMENT

I want to thank my son, Reginald Lincon, for helping me write this book.

I would also like to thank my daughter, Kimberly and my grand kids, Morgan and Jalen for inspiring me to write this book.

CHAPTER 1

Early Childhood and Family Background

A) <u>Parents and Family</u>

I was born on March 21, 1951 on the eastside of the city of Charleston, South Carolina. my parents were Christabell and John Mitchell they married at the young age of 15 When they got married they did not believed they could Have any children. After years of trying they finally got pregnant. Their first two children were boys, both boys died at a very young age. After the death of their first two Boy children, they gave birth eventually to a total of 14 other children for a total of 16 children. My father is originally from Mt Pleasant South Carolina, my mother originally from Manning, South Carolina. My parents married and settled in Charleston, South Carolina. The family is originally from Charleston, South Carolina eastside of the city of Charleston. My parents were self—employed, my parents owned and operated their own lumber wood business. They sold lumber wood to the families in the neighborhood. My parents lived and work hard in the Neighborhood. The neighborhood families loved and respected my Parents. My older siblings in the family helped my parents in the family business. During the 30s, 40s, 50s, 60s, families heated there homes with pot belly iron stoves. Which burned lumber wood inside these stoves to Heat their homes back during this period. My family was a large middle class catholic family. The family attended the neighborhood Catholic Church (Our Lady of Mercy), 2 street blocks down from the family home.

My parents were very religious and involved in the catholic faith, in which the family attended church every Sunday. My parents would place myself and my sisters and brothers in a line. The family would walk 2 street blocks down from the family home to Our Lady of Mercy catholic church religiously ever Sunday. My parents took all 16 children in the family immediately after birth to the neighborhood Catholic Church (Our Lady of Mercy). The church the family attended, to be baptized into the catholic faith. My family was a very closely religious family to this day. My entire family belong to the catholic faith (religion). Because my parents baptized myself and my sisters and brothers (siblings) into the catholic Faith immediately after birth. It became a family tradition. To date all the children, grandchildren, great grandchildren great, great grandchildren is immediately baptized into the catholic faith after birth My Parents political belief or political organization were membership of the democratic party organization in Charleston, South Carolina.

I was the third youngest child of 16 children. One of the family story told by my older sisters and brothers was how my mom caught my aunt Zenobia in bed with my father Aunt Zenobia was my mother sister I often wondered growing up why I never met my aunt Zenobia or my aunt Zenobia Children, my cousins. Aunt Zenobia lived in Albany, New York. Growing up I remember my older sister and brothers talking about my mother brother, uncle Johnny frank I never met my uncle Johnny Frank or his children, my cousins. Uncle Johnny frank lived in Los Angeles, California. The only family member of my mother I met was my mom, mother grandma daisy, who lived in Chicago, Illinois. I met my mother cousin Johnny frank. Who lived in Sumter, South Carolina the same state as the family. The family live on the eastside of the city of Charleston, South Carolina. I met grandma daisy when I was a teenager. Aunt Zenobia died so I will never meet her in my lifetime. To this Day I still have not met my father's relative, with the exception, of my father mother. I Remember my older sisters and brother talking about how mean spirited my father mother was in her older age before she died. As I tell the story about family members I never met and will never meet because they have died or left this life. it hurts especially, not meeting my father's mother my grandma alma. I also remember my older (siblings) sisters and brothers talked about how my father's dad, my grandfather disowning my father because he was born with a light complexion. Myself or my sisters and brothers never met our grandfather and to this day we have never met any of our father's relatives. My family's name is Mitchell like our dad. We will never meet our Mitchell family. I have met so many families with the Mitchell name that I will never know if we are family. That part of my family died with my father. My mom maiden name, family name was Johnson. Because I never met my mom family other than her mom, mama daisy I will never know if I am related to someone with the name Johnson. My son was in a relationship with a female friend her name was Johnson, they may have been related but the relationship ended. I met my mom cousin Johnny Frank, He has the same name as my mom brother uncle Johnny Frank. He lived in Sumter, South Carolina. He is a barber, He owned and operated his own barber shop business in Sumter, South Carolina. Cousin Johnny Frank lived in Sumter, South Carolina. My mom was born and raised in Manning, South Carolina, which is not far from Sumter, South Carolina. Cousin Johnny Frank would visit the family Occasionally. Sumter, South Carolina was no more than 100 miles from Charleston, South Carolina, Where my family lived. Growing up I have memories of my mom and my cousin Johnny Frank having very close relationship. My mom was always happy when cousin Johnny Frank would visit my mom and The family. I always admired how handsome cousin Johnny frank was during his visit with the family. I have memory of cousin Johnny Frank being tall light complexion with pretty hair.

The story in the family was that my mom had long pretty hair all the way down her back to her waist. The family story was that my mom hair caught fire and my mom ran all the way to the hospital emergency room. Growing up I have memories of the family having relative in the country. The family lived in the city of Charleston, South Carolina. If you lived in the rural area of the state out of the city limit you were Considered as living in the country (you were considered as country people). My family was city people because we lived in the city of Charleston, South Carolina. These relatives lived out of the city on an Island called Johns Island, South Carolina. (the island was dirt Dark country roads, no lights on the roads at night you can barely see your hands, snakes crawling on

The dirt roads. I am afraid of living in the country because I only knew living in the city all my life. Myself and my sisters and brothers was born and raised in the city of Charleston, South Carolina. My parents were born in the rural area of South Carolina. My dad was born and raised in Mt Pleasant, South Carolina. A rural area of South Carolina. And My mom was born and raised in Manning, South Carolina a rural area of South Carolina. Dirt dark road, no lights at night, snakes etc. Living in the City is paved roads, lighted up at night everything is within walking distance, public Transportation etc. I never seen a live snake in the city of Charleston, South Carolina where I live and grew up. I am sure snakes exist in certain area of the city of Charleston, South Carolina. Even though my parents Were born and raised in the rural area of South Carolina. I am glad they decided to settle and raise the family in the city of Charleston, South Carolina. My memory of my grandparents was limited as the third youngest of 16 Children in the family. My fondest memory of my grandma daisy my mom, mother was in my teens. When I gave birth to my son at age 18, grandma daisy and my mom assisted me with the care of my son. My grandma daisy was living with the family. She was a big help to me with my son. I was a new Teenage mom. Grandma daisy lived in Chicago, Illinois as I was growing up. Grandma daisy moved to Charleston, South Carolina from Chicago, Illinois during my teenage years. As I was growing up I always heard family stories about grandma daisy. The main story was that she always sent clothes for myself and my sibling. But that grandma daisy lived in Chicago, Illinois. Grandma daisy eventually moved away to Albany, New York to live with her daughter aunt Zenobia, my mom sister. Grandma daisy died while she was living with my aunt Zenobia. I never saw her again. Grandma daisy was the only grandparent I had the opportunity to know and spent time with before she died. My memory of my dad mom, grandma alma was that she lived with the family in her old age. And that she was very mean spirited. I have never met or have any recollection of my dad mom my grandma Alma.

I never met my mom father my grandfather or my dad father my grandfather. My understanding of Why I possibly did not meet my dad father, my grandfather was that my dad father disowned my father Because he was born light complexion. Because I did not have the opportunity of meeting my mom and My dad immediate family members like my grandfather on both my mom and my dad side of the family. I find whenever I meet or see someone with my mom last name and maiden name Johnson or someone With my family name on my dad family name Mitchell I find myself wondering if there is some Relationship.

The only ancestor I was aware of as I was growing up was my mother had a picture of this white female who Looked exactly like my baby sister Odessa. This is how I learned that the family had white blood or relative in the family. My parents had a total of 16 children 8 boys and 8 girls. I was the third youngest child, I had a Younger sister and a younger brother. As of 2016 the family only have a total of 5 children left of the 16 total children Born to my parents Christabell and John Mitchell The family has lost 9 children from 1985 to present. Along with the first 2 boy children that died at a very young age during the beginning of my parent marriage. The last 5 surviving sibling left are 4 girls and one boy my youngest brother, the baby boy of the family.

The first sibling out the nine that died in the family was my second oldest brother, his name was Gilbert Mitchell, (nick brother) he died in 1985. my brother Gilbert, growing up spoke with a stuttering, speech problem. The sibling in the family love to tease and joke one another so my brother Gilbert was the subject of jokes and teasing by his sibling on a regular basis about his stuttering speech problem. it was a part of being a member of the Mitchell family. My brother Gilbert was the second oldest brother that was very disciplinary and strict and tried to be the father figure when it came to his younger sibling or sister and brothers. He was very short patient. If you made him angry he would stutter with speech and would attempt to hit you.

You would have to run to get away from him. He especially, acted like a father figure to his younger Sisters and brothers after daddy died. He eventually, got married, in the family home town of Charleston, South Carolina. Him and his wife adopted his wife nephew William. They moved to Albany, New York where my oldest brother William, oldest sister Hermine, her husband Roscoe and their kids and my second oldest sister

Zenobia lived. After moving to Albany, New York his wife gave birth to 3 girls and 2 boys. The youngest boy was named after our father John. My brother and his family moved back to Charleston, South Carolina. After living in Albany, New York for about 20 years. After living back home in Charleston, South Carolina for 4 years he separated from his wife and kids. His wife decided to take my brother to family court to pay child support. My brother could not find a job. He became delinquent on his child support. to keep from going to jail for none payment of his child support payments. He returned to Albany, New York. about a year after returning to Albany, New York. He died, he was either thrown or fell from a 5th floor window to his death. My mom, my brother and his wife had just arrived in New York they were on vacation headed to visit my oldest sister Hermine, who also lived in Albany, New York. When they received the telephone call about my brother Gilbert death After receiving the telephone call about my brother Gilbert death, they went to the New York city morgue to claim my brother Gilbert body. when my mom, my brother and his wife arrived at the morgue. There was this couple at the morgue claiming my brother Gilbert body at the same time. My family is still not sure how my brother Gilbert died. Was he thrown or fell from that 5th floor window.

The second oldest brother that died in the family was my oldest brother. His name was William Mitchell My oldest brother William left home and went in the military. When I was about 5 years old. My memory of my brother William was from family stories as I was growing up. My memory is My brother William left to join the military. He met his wife, they married and had 5 girl children. They settled in Long Island, New York. My brother and his wife was determined to have a Boy child. His wife name was Ann. She finally, got pregnant after years of trying to have a boy. When Ann finally got pregnant. She had complication during child birth. My brother wife Ann and the boy baby she Was carrying died in child birth. My brother and his mother-in-law, his wife mother continued to raise My brother William 5 girl children. My brother daughters were very young girls when my brother wife Ann died. I heard about my brother and his girls over the years as I grew up. My last memory of My oldest brother William was about age 5 when he left home to join the military. I heard stories of his life from family members. My sister Bernadette left the family home town. Of Charleston, South Carolina as a teenager to live with my oldest brother William, his girls, his wife Ann and Mother-in-law patty. My sister Bernadette lived with our oldest brother William and his family until she graduated High school. After completing high school, my sister Bernie returned back to the family home town of Charleston, South Carolina. Before my brother wife Ann became pregnant with my brother William and his wife boy child. I remember when my sister Bernie returned home. Because she is 3 years older than I am. She was 18 when she graduated I was 15 years old. I remember that my sister Bernadette favorite words when she returned home was (every time the family was at the dinner table after my sister Bernadette got through eating, she would just yell out "Um boy that was good" at the Dinner table). After my oldest brother, William wife Ann died his mother-in-law patty who was staying with my brother William and his family, help raised her granddaughters her daughter Ann kids. The Stories told among the family and because my brother oldest daughter Amanda is in contact with the Family. My oldest brother William kids is all grown up as of today and living their own lives. My family buried my oldest brother William in 1995.

Myself and my sisters and brothers drove to Long Island, New York to my oldest brother William funeral. My third oldest brother Walter was in charge of the family trip to my oldest brother William funeral. My brother Walter son was driving the vehicle the family rented to attend the funeral. He missed the turn off on the way to my brother William home. My brother Walter was in charge of the trip and the vehicle the family was being transported in to my oldest brother William house. His son was driving the vehicle and missed the turn off to my brother William house but my brother Walter who was in charge made the family drive around for hours paying toll after toll refusing to let the family stop and ask for advice to my brother William house. When the family finally arrived at my brother William house for his funeral everyone was so tired. I just said let me out this vehicle now. When we got to my brother house the family finally got a chance to meet my brother William daughters for the first time. they were grown Women. The family also got a chance to meet my brother mother-in-law Patty, the girl's grandmother. who helped my brother raise his 5 girls. My brother was gone from this life and his girls but I am sure he was resting in peace knowing his kids even thought they were grown women was still in good hands. with their grandmother Patty, his wife Ann's mother. who help raised them all their lives and who took the place of their mother Ann at a young age when their mother died. The day after the family arrived at my oldest brother William house. My sister Odessa had everyone on the floor laughing at her jokes. to this day, I could still remember my sister Odessa sitting on my brother William couch with her legs up in the air laughing at her on jokes. Drinking and socializing. If my brother William could have seen the family joking and laughing as the family did as he grew up, he would have had just as much fun laughing. This was a trip to pay respect to my oldest brother William and his death but the family members that had not seen one another in years, a long time, got the opportunity to spend lost time together, they had not spent in years. This is a death in a family, a sad time, but death in every family bring about sadness. But my oldest brother William death brought family members that had not seen one another, together to see one another and spent time that was never spent again. I never saw some of these family members again. They left this life like my sister Hermine who just recently died and her husband who took his life. Who took a gun and shot himself in the head a month after my sister Hermine death, his wife of 40 years died in 2000. I never saw my brother girls again with the exception, of my brother William oldest daughter Amanda who came down to spend time with the family. My brother William died in 1995 of a heart attack after his wife death in 1965 in child birth. I was told that my oldest brother William Mitchell was a loving husband and father. When my father died, he and my brothers helped My mom with myself and my sisters and brothers. My siblings always spoke of my oldest brothers as protective of his siblings. And that he was quiet.

My parents John and Christabell Mitchell gave birth to 16 kids 8 boys and 8 girls. The first 2 boys died at a very young age. The first 2 death at the beginning of my parent marriage was the first death in the family. The next death in the family was my father's death in 1960 I was 9 years old. My father John Mitchell was admitted to South Carolina State Mental Hospital as a patient in 1960 because of his obsessive alcohol consumption. My father was killed in the state mental hospital by another mental patient while he was a patient. This mental patient bash my father head in and killed him. My mom Christabell Mitchell died in December 23, 1989 just before Christmas of that year. My mama body was laying inside the morgue for Christmas. In 1985 my second oldest brother Gilbert Mitchell died after Possibly thrown from a 5ᵗʰ story building in Albany, New York. The next death in the family was in 1995 my oldest brother William Mitchell died of a heart attack. In the year 2000 my oldest sister Hermine died in Albany, New York of a sudden death. They say death sometimes comes in threes. The family seem to have one death after another. My oldest Sister Hermine died in 2000. She was found dead in her home in Albany New York. She was found by her husband they were married for at least 30 to 40 years. They Had grown kids and grandkids. After she died her Husband took a gun and put it to his head and Killed himself. They had 2 girls, and 1 boy they adopted a son. But when they both died, the kids Were in their 20s and 30s. My sister Hermine before she left the family home town of Charleston, South Carolina in the 1950s after getting married to her husband when I was about 5 years old. She moved Away from Charleston, South Carolina to Albany, New York because her mother-in-law was against her Marriage to her husband and the story among the family for years was that her mother—in-law believed in witch craft and she used it on my sister Hermine because she did not want or respected the decision of my oldest sister Hermine and her husband to marry. My sister Hermine was the oldest sister (sibling) out of the 8 girls my mom gave birth. I remember being the third youngest child. I had a younger sister and a younger brother. My sister Hermine was like the siblings in the family second mama. My Sister Hermine was the oldest sibling and because there were so many children in the family, my oldest sister Hermine had to help my parents with the younger siblings. My parents had 2 two story homes, the homes were sided by side next door to each other. The family lived in one and the other home was rented to tenants. Both homes were two story homes, upstairs and downstairs. The house my parents Rented out to tenants had two stories upstairs and downstairs. My parents rented the upstairs out to one family and the downstairs to another family. The house that the family stayed in there was a big tree in the backyard of the family home. The family home was upstairs and down stairs (2story Home). The way the family home was designed upstairs was the bedrooms and restrooms and downstairs was the kitchen on the downstairs back end of the family home and dining room and living room was also down stairs but you could see the backyard from the back downstairs of the house which was the kitchen. So, the kids in the family would play in the backyard of the family home. And my oldest sister Hermine (the kids in the family second mama) would be watching the younger Kids playing in the backyard from the back part of the family home, the kitchen. She would tell The younger siblings not to play or swing on the big tree in the backyard of the family home but Myself and my younger siblings would sneak and play and swing on this big tree in the back area Of the family home backyard. My oldest sister Hermine (second mama) would be watching from the Back kitchen area to make sure we did not disobey her and swing on the tree called the weeping willow Tree. When we disobey her as the oldest sister (second mama), she would run out of the back kitchen Door into the family home back yard with a belt trying to catch us younger siblings, to beat or discipline Us younger sibling with a belt. This was my memory of my oldest sister. Before she got married and Move to Albany, New York where she never move back home. She only visited the family over the years. But my oldest sister Hermine not only was the disciplinary of the younger siblings, who help my mom Take care of her younger siblings, especially, after my dad died in 1960. All my older siblings assisted My mom with the younger siblings. My parents gave birth to 16 children, after the first two boys died The family consisted of 14 family siblings, which was hard for one parent or even two parent to have to Control and take care. But my sister Hermine was very heroic. I was one of the younger siblings. The Story was from my older siblings was daddy started drinking and became an alcoholic and started being Physically violent towards my mom over the years. (I was the third youngest child, my memory of my father as a child is my older brothers taking my father out the family home. four of my brothers carrying my father. four of my brother carrying my father each have a leg or arm) The family story went that My sister Hermine Jumped in front of my mom one day when daddy was under the influence of alcohol and attempted to take a gun and tried to shoot my mom. My oldest sister Hermine took a bullet for my mama. She survived the shooting. The bullet was never removed but she lived a full life. My sister Hermine and her husband after moving away from the family home Town of Charleston, South Carolina to Albany, New York was very successful. My oldest sister Hermine and her husband they bought apartment Buildings, they rented to tenants, they bought machines that was used to remove the snow off the Streets of New York, they bought a huge house for their family in a nice neighborhood, they Were Wealthy before they died. My oldest sister(sibling) Hermine Mitchell save my mama life. When she jumped in front of my mama.

Before she got married, left Charleston, South Carolina and moved to Albany, New York To start her life with her husband. But the story told in the family by my sister Sylvia Scott another older Siblings (sister). That just before my mama died and when my mama was sick. My sister Sylvia called My sister Hermine to ask her to call mama because she was sick, my sister Sylvia said that my sister Hermine told my sister Sylvia that she would Call my mama her mama, who was sick, that she would call her mama as a favor to my sister Sylvia. My older sister Hermine apparently had turned bitter toward my mama her mama for her own Personal reasons.

My brother Walter was the third oldest brother of 6 living brothers growing up. My first two brothers when my parents first got married died. at a young age. Before I was born. My third oldest brother Walter along with my other older (siblings) sisters and brothers assisted or helped my mama with the care of the younger siblings, especially after my father died. My brothers dropped out of school after My father died to help my mother with the other siblings especially, after my dad left my mother with 14 children to raise. My third oldest brother Walter was tight with money. And he was very strict and protective when it came to his Mother and his siblings. If you disrespected his female siblings. My third oldest brother Walter went in the military while he was in the military, he got Married to his wife who lived in the family home town of Charleston, South Carolina. My third oldest brother Walter and his wife had a total of two girls and three boy children in their marriage. He worked at a lumber Company after he left the military. Later, he worked at the College of Charleston, Charleston, South Carolina. As a state security officer. He left the College of Charleston and took a job with Medical University Hospital, Charleston, South Carolina. As a state security officer in Charleston, South Carolina where he eventually, retired. After he Retired, from Medical University Hospital as a state security officer as a result of a heart condition which lead to numerous heart attacks, Because he could not work, he drove taxi cab for the extra Income.

My mom came down with diabetes in 1956 when I was 5 years old. I believe that I was the only Sibling in the family that did not have diabetes. My doctor told me that the only reason I did not Have diabetes was because I exercise for years. I still exercise to this day 2017. My third oldest brother Walter Before he died. Had diabetes. He also had a heart condition. In which he had to have a pace—maker surgically inserted in his heart. My brother Walter before he died. He suffered with diabetes and Heart Problem for years but a month after he was diagnosed with cancer he died. In February 2001, My four oldest brother Gerald, who was a brother always telling jokes, and having the other sisters and brothers laughing. He made the statement after my third oldest brother Walter's death. He made the statement. "I wonder who will be next," he meant which of the remaining family member will be the next to die and he laughed. The family had just left my third oldest brother Walter grave site and returned to my brother Walter home to pay the family respect to his wife and kids. After my brother Gerald made that statement, "I wonder who will be next" meaning I wonder which of the remaining family member will be the next to die. He laughed and all the remaining sisters and brothers laughed but because the siblings in the family knew his personality and took everything my brother Gerald said as a joke and funny. The remaining siblings and family member just laughed at my brother Gerald next joke and did not think twice about the statement my brother Gerald had made we just laughed at his next joke because that was his personality as we knew him all his life. My brother Gerald was one of my siblings that had the Mitchell trade mark. My mama Christabell had the family trade mark she had a funny sense of humor and she pasted it down to her children and some of the children in the family have a stronger family trade mark to make the people around them laugh than the other siblings in the family. I inherited zero of the Family trade mark from my mama to make people laugh. I try to be funny but I don't have the family trade mark from our mama. But I know for sure that if my brother Gerald knew or had a clue that he would be the next sibling out of the remaining sister and brother in the family to die or his funeral would be the next funeral the family plan he would not have made that joke or statement of "I wonder who will be next." In which he made a joke as to who will be the next remaining sibling in the family to die. He was the next sibling to die. He did not know that he was next. I have always heard the term or statement, "no fool no fun" or "The life of the party" My fourth oldest brother Gerald had the family trade mark inherited from our mama Christabell Mitchell because The children in the family grew up with our mother funny sense of humor. which was inherited by all the children in the Mitchell family except me I was left out. I try to be funny over the years but it just does not happen for me, But my brother Gerald and some of my other siblings inherited my mama family trade mark to make the people around them laugh. But my brother Gerald made other people over the years the subject of his jokes but before he left this life. His own joke that he made as to who out of the remaining children in the family will be the next to die was on Him and he did not realize it.

My baby sister Odessa left home when she was about 18 years old she left the family hometown of Charleston, South Carolina to go to New York to live with our oldest brother William Mitchell. He was Married and lived in Long Island, New York before my baby sister could get to long Island New York to My brother home. The story was that she never made it to my oldest brother William home in Long Island, New York. The story in the family was that when she stepped of the grey hound bus in New York this man who, the family referred to as (Pimp) Kidnapped her and made her into his woman of the night for years. The family could not get her back for years, she had two kids, my mom Raised her daughter and son. She gave birth to a daughter in which he was the child father after About 20 years he finally allowed my sister to come back home but he would not allow her to bring her Daughter with her. She came back home stayed with my mom and her daughter and son. She eventually Met a man began a relationship and gave birth to a daughter and a son. She got her own Apartment in Charleston, South Carolina the family home town. She developed a relationship with her Older children my mom raised. Finally, we had my baby sister back home. My baby sister Odessa kidnaper had her on drugs. My baby sister

Odessa participated in a substance abuse treatment program and finally became free of drugs. My baby sister Odessa had such a hilarious fun loving comedian personality the family Trade Mark. Whenever the family had gatherings, my baby sister would have everyone at the party or in the room on the floor laughing at her jokes. Like the old saying "no fool no fun," or "the life of the party" she was the fool at the party or the family gatherings that made everyone laugh. My baby sister Odessa was back home 20 years later. Her younger kids were up in age when she became sick with kidney failure. Both her kidney failed, five years she suffered with kidney failure and went to dialysis treatment for kidney failure. 5 years before she went in a nursing home and finally died in the hospital. When she was a patient in the nursing home. Her daughter thought that she was bothersome, so, one night in the nursing home she got sick. The nursing home took her to the hospital late that night while in the hospital dying, she called her daughter, she did not answer her phone, thinking my baby sister Odessa was being bothersome (the nursing home should have notified the family) My baby sister died that night in the hospital by herself with all the family she had in Charleston, South Carolina none of the family knew she had died. The nursing home did not inform the family. My baby sister Odessa body laid up in the Medical University Hospital, Charleston, South Carolina morgue for a week no one in the family Knew my baby sister Odessa had died. Until someone who knew the family came by my third oldest sister Mary home and told her that my baby sister Odessa had died and was laying up in the Medical University Hospital Charleston, South Carolina morgue for a week.

Before my baby sister Odessa died she attended our oldest brother William Mitchell funeral in 1995 along with the family in Long Island, New York. My baby sister Odessa and I went to the neighborhood grocery store in my oldest brother William Mitchell Neighborhood. when we went to my oldest brother funeral in 1995 to get some beer for the family members. when my baby sister Odessa and myself left my brother William neighborhood grocery store to head back to my brother William house. My baby sister told me she was going to walk to catch the New York transit system (the subway to go look for her daughter that she was force to leave with her kidnaper. Because he was my baby sister Odessa daughter's father.

When he finally allowed my sister Odessa to come back home after 20 years later to the family but he did not allow my sister Odessa to come home with my sister Odessa daughter. The daughter that my baby sister Odessa children or family back in the family home town of Charleston, South Carolina still has not met. My baby sister Odessa turned around and decide not to catch Th New York transit system (the subway) to go look for her daughter she was force to leave with her daughter father in New York when she returned back home after being away from the family for 20 years. My baby sister Odessa changed her mind about trying to catch the subway to go look for her daughter she left in New York with her daughter father that she was not allow to bring home with her when she returned home to the family in the family home town of the City of Charleston, South Carolina. My baby sister Odessa and I took the beer we bought from the grocery store in my brother William neighborhood went back to my brother William house. where my sisters and brothers and family members that came to attend my brother William funeral were gathered. My sister Odessa began Portraying the family trade mark, she inherited from my mama. My sister Odessa began joking and teasing all the family member that was at my brother William house. She was sitting on my brother William couch laughing at her own jokes with her legs in the air and drinking the beer we had just bought from the neighborhood grocery store, my baby sister Odessa had everyone at my brother William house on the floor laughing their behinds off. My sister Odessa made the stay at my brother house for my brother funeral so much fun. Especially my brother daughters and mother-in-law who had never met or experienced my sister Odessa personality before. My other siblings that was also at my brother William house who had the family trade mark to make the people around them laugh. My sister Zenobia, my brother Richard, my brother Walter, my sister Bernadette, my sister Louise, My sister Sylvia, my baby brother Andrew, my oldest sister Hermine I am sure if my brother William was alive and had not died he would have been a part of the family trade mark pasted down by our mother to make the people around us laugh. Instead of catching the subway to look for her daughter my sister Odessa ended up drinking the beer we bought from the neighborhood store and getting drunk along with the family and having the Fun we as sibling and family growing up use to having at the family gatherings. The family gatherings were always consisted of lot of uncontrollable laughter and fun. Some of the family members at my brother William house and funeral died and left this life. This was 1995 my oldest sister Hermine in the year 2000 her husband Roscoe found her in their home dead. A month later in 2000 after 40 years of marriage my sister Hermine husband Roscoe I guess he could not accept his wife Hermine death, He place a gun to his head and blew his brain out. This was the first time I saw my brother William 5 girls I have not had the opportunity to see my brother girls again with the exception of the oldest daughter Amanda who visited the family.

My brother Gerald Roscoe Mitchell was my fourth oldest brother. He died in 2006. My brother Gerald like my other older sibling help my parents with their self-employed lumber Wood business and when daddy died, he dropped out school to work at the corner grocery store, Henry's grocery, on the corner from the family home. To help my mother with the younger children (siblings) in the family. The family buried my brother Walter in February 2001 after the family left my third oldest brother Walter burial site and went back to my brother Walter home to pay the family respect to my third oldest brother Walter family. My brother Gerald made the statement jokingly that I wonder who will be next." Who will be the remaining family member to die. He did not know that his funeral would be the next funeral the family held. The saying, "no fool, no fun" or the life of the party," is a good description of my brother Gerald. Every one of my sisters and brothers had the family trade mark they were the Life of the party, they knew how to joke and tease you so hard that everyone would be laughing so hard that they would be on the floor with tears in their eyes, wetting their pants and their stomach hurting from laughing so hard. It was a trade mark of the Mitchell family because My mom had a sense of humor. I was the quiet sibling. I don't know how to explain my brother Gerald. I was the third youngest child but I remember my brother Gerald. As playing the piano and singing as I grew up as a child. Because my parents had a piano downstairs in the family home dining room as I was growing up. Everyone in the family though my brother Gerald would be a singer. Ever since. I was old enough to remember as a younger sibling. My brother Gerald had me and my siblings laughing so hard, on the floor in tears, and literally wetting our pants and stomach hurting from so much laughter. My brother Gerald was a nutty, fun loving person. Everything came out his mouth was funny. He was someone who could tell a joke about you and everyone would think it was funny. He probably could have been a comedian. Everyone like being in his company. He was always the life of the party of all the family gatherings. He made family gatherings over the years so much fun. My brother Gerald worked at the corner grocery store, Henry's grocery. This is where he met his wife. They got married and had a daughter. He was a young man. He was in love with his wife but one day, he decided to leave his job henry's grocery to go home for lunch, he lived close to henry's grocery store his job. But when he got home, he found his young wife in bed with another man. Being young and in love with his wife it destroyed his life. He never trusted another woman or got married ever again. Every woman He met caught hell and was a "broke up pussy bitch" for the rest of his life. He began drinking alcohol and sometimes when he drank too much alcohol and if he is at my mom house, he would sometimes curse my mom out and have been known to call my mom a "broke up pussy bitch." He was eventually in a relationship with another woman years later, she had a daughter for him but he never married her. She met and got married to another man in the military and her husband adopted my brother Gerald daughter. My brother Gerald died in the hospital intensive care unit. Prior, to my brother Gerald death he made a statement "I wonder who will be next" after my third oldest brother Walter funeral in February 2001. It's ironic that he was the next sibling or family member to die. But when he made that statement he did not know the family would be burying him next after my brother Walter funeral. What lead up to my brother Gerald death in 2006. In 2005, he went in the hospital in Charleston, South Carolina and underwent intestinal bowl surgery. In 2006 his bowel became obstructed, he went to Charleston County Memorial Hospital, Charleston, South Carolina Emergency Room. The doctors, as a result of my brother Gerald seeking medical care at Charleston County Memorial Hospital Charleston, South Carolina for Bowel obstruction. The emergency room doctor decision to perform emergency intestinal bowel surgery to relieve his bowel obstruction. Because his body was not physically healthy enough for the surgery his body went in to shock and his organs shut down. His organs shut down. His lung, heart and kidney shut down on him he went into a comma. The family did not know about the surgery. Until week or two weeks after the surgery when his neighbors notice that his mail was backing up. At his apartment and decided to go to my third oldest sister Mary house and alarm her. She decided to call around and she found out that he was in the intensive care unit at Medical University hospital, Charleston, South Carolina in a comma and had been in intensive care for two weeks on life support, as a result of the Charleston Memorial Hospital Charleston, South Carolina decision to do emergency surgery. The family began to visit my brother Gerald for weeks and prayed that my brother Gerald would get better. The family felt he was getting better. He was never taken of life support. He could not speak to tell the family exactly what happen. The tube was never taken out his throat. So, he could not talk to the family. My nephew got shot 5 times and was in the intensive care unit with my brother Gerald. The family though our nephew would have died after being shot 5 times but my nephew recovered and my brother organs began to fail his lungs failed because he had walking pneumonia in his lungs for years. He had already had two, three heart attacks, his kidney failed. The only organ that had not failed was his liver. The doctors called the family to the hospital to explain that all his organs had failed and that he had already had at least 3 heart attacks. The doctors explained that the only organ that had not failed was his liver. The doctors wanted to know should my brother Gerald have another heart attack should the doctor resuscitate. In order, to try to keep my brother Gerald alive on life support. His daughter made the decision not to resuscitate if he had another heart attack the family gathered around my brother Gerald hospital bed that morning and prayed together for my fourth oldest brother Gerald but that night I went to visit my brother only to walk in his hospital room to see the nurse having gauge in his nose and suctioning blood out his mouth. She had him hooked up to plasma of blood to replace the blood that was coming out every part of his body.

My brother Gerald last organ had failed and shut down he no longer had any working organs in his body. His liver had failed. The liver is what clots the blood in your body. His body had no more working organs when his liver shut down. He had no blood clothing mechanism to keep the blood from flow from his body. My brother Gerald needed these failed organs to keep his body functioning and to keep him alive. I called my family they were arguing with me about coming to the hospital. I was having a hard time convincing them to come to the hospital. I had the nurse talked to them over phone to get them to see the seriousness of my brother Gerald condition but it seemed they were more interested in giving me a hard way to go on the phone. I called my daughter, explain what was going on and she told me to call my son to be with me. My daughter lived in Jacksonville, Florida My son Reginald and I lived in the family home town of Charleston, South Carolina. I called my son and explain what was going on and told him that I would come pick him up from home. When I got on the hospital elevator to go pick my son up my sisters that I spoke with over the phone had decided to come to the hospital after my telephone conversation with them. They were on the hospital elevator as I was leaving the hospital to go pick up my son to have him stay at the hospital with me over night with my brother Gerald. My family members once at the hospital decided they did not want my brother Gerald to suffer any longer they brought my brother Gerald daughter with them to the hospital to make the Final decisions for her dying father.

My brother Gerald daughter decision was to disconnect my brother her father from the life support that night and the family watch him take his last breath that was the first time I saw someone take their last breath. The family was expecting our nephew not to make it but my nephew had already been shot 6 time prior to being shot 5 times this time. My nephew made it out the hospital and is healthy today. He has a lot of bullet holes in his body but he is healthy and our brother Gerald died.

My sister Mary was the third oldest sister (sibling) out of 8 girls in the family. She died in 2011. She died Of cancer of the liver. She was taken to Medical University Hospital, Charleston, South Carolina Emergency room. By her daughter because she was too sick to get out of bed. Medical University Hospital, Charleston, South Carolina ordered a series of tests on my sister Mary. The diagnoses Was that she had a tumor on her liver the size of a grapefruit. Her weight loss was so tremendous that she looked like a skeleton. After her stay in the hospital for her diagnosis and treatment. She was told by the doctors that they could not do anything else for her.

She was sent home to die. She was not given any prior notice. She was simply told by the doctors that she had a month to live. My third oldest sister was seen as a patient by her regular physician. She always kept her appointments. She was always healthy. My sister Mary was being seen as a patient for years by her regular physician prior to her being diagnosed with cancer of the liver. My third oldest sister Mary was diagnosed by Medical University Hospital, Charleston, South Carolina with Cancer. My sister Mary were taken toMedical University Hospital, Charleston, South Carolina Emergency room. In which she was diagnosed and treated for cancer and sent home to die. She was told by Medical University Hospital doctors there was nothing else they could do for her. She was not only seen as a patient by her regular physician in Charleston, South Carolina for years. My Sister Mary was going back and forth to her regular physician as a patient in Charleston, South Carolina complaining that the medication that her doctor Prescribed and treated her with was not working. I was told that my sister Mary was actually taking the medicine she was prescribed by her doctor in Charleston, South Carolina back to her doctor because the medication that was prescribed for her was not making her feel better. I heard that her daughter was also concern and went to her doctor on her mother behalf. The doctors at Medical University Hospital,Charleston, South Carolina explained to the family that in order for my sister Mary tumor on her liver to be the size of a grapefruit. My sister Mary tumor on her liver had to been growing for years. The doctor explained that the tumor on my sister Mary liver had pretty much taken over her liver. My sister was sent home to die. She was given a month to live. After being taken to the emergency room by her daughter because she was feeling weak.

She had lost a lot of weight. her body weight was the size of a skeleton. I called the cancer center for advice. After, the Medical University Hospital, Charleston, South Carolina sent my sister Mary home to die in a month. The cancer Center Told me that my sister Mary weight loss was a sign of cancer. If I notice the skeletal weight loss of my third oldest sister Mary while she was a patient for her treatment and diagnosis at Medical University Hospital, Charleston, South Carolina. My sister Mary doctor should have notice the tremendous weight loss. My sister Mary doctor did not have an ultra sound or x-ray machine. They did not have a machine to look in Inside a patient body to see if they have internal injury or medical complication inside their body. Most doctors normally, refer their patients out. If they did not have the medical machinery or facility to treat the patient. My sister Mary doctor should have referred my sister Mary out for more extensive test. The question is why my sister Mary not referred out for more testing. The family was given a month to say their good bye to a sibling (sister) who has mean the world to them. She was the sister, mom, grandmother, great grandmother, great, great, grandmother the aunt. That everyone in the family loved, depended on and look up to be there, if no one else was there. I remember when I was in labor with my daughter Kimberly in the hospital at Medical University Hospital, Charleston, South Carolina. I was given a doctor's appointment to the clinic at Medical University Hospital because I was two weeks late. I kept my appointment after the doctor examine me the doctor decided to admit me and induce my labor. I was giving birth to my daughter. I was going to go into labor and have my daughter at the last minute. I was already in the hospital Because I was transferred from the Medical University Hospital clinic to the labor room. I needed someone to keep my 13 years old son. I called my sister Mary I told her I was in the hospital in labor and I needed her to keep my son. She was arguing on the phone with me that she was not going to keep my son. She had no choice. I was in labor and I could not leave the hospital in labor. She knew she was going to keep him. She knew I could not leave the labor room because I was giving birth to my daughter. But she argued with me. She was the sister that everybody in the family turned to be there whenever there was a situation Going on in the family. She was the go to person for the family. Her house was the family hang out Especially, after mama died. She was the oldest sister in the family home town, Charleston, South Carolina. My other older siblings, sisters and brothers lived in New York. She would argue and said She would not be there for her siblings but she was always there (my mom died in 1989, my mom always told her children no matter how old they were that she was not going to be there for them but like my third oldest sister Mary she argued and said she would not be there but she always was there. This was true for all my older siblings, especially, after my father died and left my mama with 14 kids to raise. My sister Mary died at home in her down stairs living room in a hospital bed the family watched her pass away.

My family is catholic I would have preferred the priest giving my sister Mary the last rights and praying over her as she took her last breath. But her husband did not want the priest called again. The priest had already prayed with my sister Mary before she died. My sister Louise and I prayed the rosary over my third oldest sister Mary as she took her last breath. My sister Mary kids weren't with their mother when she took her last breath. They could not watch her take her last breath. They were given such short notice of their mother death. When my sister Mary was in the hospital, Medical University hospital Charleston, South Carolina my sister Mary daughter Ronda, (she was name after her dad) took my sister her mom to the Emergency Room. When my sister was admitted in the hospital from the emergency room my niece Ronda never left her mother's side. She did not even go home to change her clothes. She was eventually replaced by her cousin, who was a nurse. My sister Mary had just buried her 5 years old granddaughter, who had suffered with a brain tumor a month or two earlier. She buried her granddaughter not knowing that she had a tumor on her liver that was growing for years and that the family and her husband and children would be planning her funeral next.

My sister Zenobia Daisy Mitchell was the second oldest girl in the family. My sister Zenobia was named after my grandmother, my mother mom, grandma Daisy and my mama sister Zenobia My sister Zenobia died in 2012. My sister Zenobia got married at a very young age. She got Married one day and her husband went to jail the very next day for robbery. Her marriage Was never official. My sister Zenobia eventually decided to move to Albany, New York. Where My oldest sister Hermine Mitchell Richardson and her husband lived. My sister Zenobia settled down In Albany, New York. She met her kids father. My sister Zenobia had a total of 2 boys and 2 girls for her Kids father. My sister Zenobia and my sister Hermine my 2 oldest sisters settled down and decided to Start a family in Albany, New York. My sisters only came home for family funerals and occasional visits. Prior, to my sister Zenobia death, she had move back home for about 3-4 years. Her kids were grown But she decided to move back to Albany, New York because she was unable to find employment back Home in the family home town of Charleston, South Carolina. When my second oldest sister moved back to Albany, New York her oldest daughter Karen died about 3-4 years after she returned to Albany, New York. My sister Zenobia daughter Karen was a victim of Albany, New York police officer brutality. The Story is that my sister Zenobia oldest daughter Karen my niece was shopping with her 14 year Old daughter, when the police officer confronted my 14 years old niece, my grandniece said something. The Albany, New York police officer did not like. Because she was 14 years old and out with her mother Karen. My sister Zenobia daughter Karen confronted the police officer for placing her daughter in the Police car because my grandniece was only 14 years old and being placed in the police car her mother My sister Zenobia daughter Karen, confronted the police officer about putting her 14 years old daughter In the police car. The police officer placed my sister Zenobia daughter Karen in a choke hold. My niece Karen later went to the hospital for treatment. Days later after my sister Zenobia oldest daughter Karen Left the hospital after treatment. She was found dead in her bed. When her daughter went to Wake her mom up. My sister Zenobia was very close to her oldest daughter Karen. She was a young mother. My sister Zenobia took custody of my niece Karen children. But she never recovered from her daughter Karen death. My sister Zenobia gave birth to two boys and 2 girls, she was very close to her two girls Tara her baby And Karen the oldest girl. But her boys seem to have trouble with the law. When she died Both her boys were in jail. I saw my 2nd oldest sister Zenobia when she came home in 2009 for my third oldest sister Mary Funeral. My sister Zenobia attended our third oldest sister Mary funeral. not knowing her funeral was Going to be the next funeral the family plan and held. My sister Zenobia died in 2012 two years after she came Home to our third oldest sister Mary Funeral. My family like I said early was full of siblings that knew how to joke and tease you so hard that everyone would be on the floor laughing so hard there is tears, wetting their pants and their stomach hurting from so much laughter. My sister Zenobia had the Mitchell family trade mark. She knew how to make the people around her laugh. Like the saying goes "no fool no fun" or "the life of the party" this was a good description of my second oldest sister Zenobia. My sister Zenobia was my 2nd oldest sister. When my sister was still living in my mother house as a young adult dating, she would use the hot Iron that you use to iron your clothes with to iron her hair to striating her hair out.

She would press her hair out before she went on a date. The family had four siblings that knew how to make everyone laugh so hard that they were on the floor laughing to tears and wetting their pants. They were my baby sister Odessa, my 2nd oldest sister Zenobia, My fourth oldest brother Gerald and My fourth older sister Bernadette. My other sisters and brothers knew how to make you laugh but They were not as funny as my sister Bernadette, Odessa, Gerald and Zenobia. I totally don't have the family trade mark I try to make people laugh like my siblings but I don't have it. I grew up a complete introvert I was afraid to go to people's house I knew. afraid I would not have anything to say. I grew up the quite sibling in the Mitchell family. My brother Gerald would say if you "Grin you in, that mean you might be the next person he might tease or joke about. My sister Zenobia my 2nd oldest sister, she would tell you That you might be the next to be tease also like my brother Gerald. These siblings were the life of the Party. When my sister Zenobia, went back to Albany, New York after attending my sister. Mary funeral. She went in the county hospital in Albany, New York for a medical problem she was experiencing. Before the hospital released her my sister Zenobia told the doctors that she was not feeling well enough to be released but the hospital personnel released my sister Zenobia from the hospital in spite, of her telling the hospital personnel that she needed to stay in the hospital because she did not feel well enough to be released. The hospital released my sister Zenobia from the hospital.

The following week her daughter Tara took, my sister Zenobia to another appointment at a different Hospital. While my sister Zenobia was waiting to be seen for her appointment she went into cardiac Arrest in the waiting area of the hospital. The hospital attempted to treat her for cardiac arrest But because the medical team nurses, doctors, whoever worked on my sister Zenobia took too long to Revive her from her cardiac arrest. Which left my sister Zenobia brain dead and in a coma. My second oldest sister Zenobia never survived. She was on life support the machine was breathing for her, she was brain dead. The life support machine was keeping her alive. Because my sister Zenobia told her daughter Tara her baby daughter, that if she was ever on life support do not take her of life support. when my niece had to decide whether to take her mama, my sister Zenobia of life support she could not do it. The doctors explain to Tara my niece that her mom was brain dead. She felt the doctors was pressuring her to disconnect Her mom from the life support machine. My niece Tara was all along in Albany, New York she was married and she had her husband to help with their son but her brother was in jail and they could not help her make decisions. The family at home in the family home town of Charleston, South Carolina did not go to Albany, New York to be there for her. So, my niece Tara placed her mom my sister Zenobia in a nursing home. Where my sister Zenobia, about a year later, died from bed sores and a blood infection my sister Zenobia was diagnosed with when my second oldest sister Zenobia was released from that first hospital (Albany, New York County Hospital). That first Hospital should not have release my sister Zenobia. She should not have been released because She had a blood infection that caused my sister Zenobia to go into cardiac arrest the following week.

While she was in the waiting area waiting to be seen the following week at a private hospital. My sister Zenobia was my 2nd oldest sister (sibling) she helped provide for me and my younger siblings Especially after my daddy died. And left my mama with 14 kids to raise. I miss my family members that Have left this world dearly.

My brother Richard Mitchell was the fifth older brother, he died in 2009 from lung cancer.

My brother suffered with lung cancer for 10 years before he died. His cancer over the years spread From his lungs, to his spine, and eventually before he died the cancer had spread to the bones in his legs. In 2009 before my brother died. After suffering for so long with cancer. My brother finally, made up his Mind. He told his wife that he was tired of depending on people. He went to the Medical university Hospital, Charleston, South Carolina. He told the doctors if he had a cardiac arrest do not resuscitate. He was ready to die. He had finally, resigned himself. After 10 years of suffering and struggling with Cancer he did not want to live any longer. After my brother got to the hospital, Medical University Hospital, Charleston, South Carolina. My brother wife began calling family to the hospital and the family Members that was at the hospital started calling other family members to the hospital. My son Reginald And I was the last called to the hospital. My brother Richard had an outside child. Her name was April. April mother and my brother had a relationship outside my brother marriage. My brother and his Wife was married for 40 years, before he died. But my brother Richard and his wife Shirley did not have Kids together. When they met, his wife Shirley had a 2 years old daughter. Before they got married. Her name was Bonnie(boo). My brother adopted Bonnie after his marriage to Bonnie mother Shirley. But my brother wife Shirley found out about her husband Richard my brother outside daughter April and his relationship with his daughter mother. Because Shirley my brother wife did not have any kids for my brother her husband My brother wife Shirley hated April my brother outside daughter. So, when my brother was sick from cancer, April his daughter offered to help my brother wife Shirley with my brother her father care. Shirley my brother wife would not let April my brother outside daughter help take care or see her daddy. My brother had to see his daughter on his own time and way. So, when my brother was dying and all the family was being called to the hospital to say their good byes to my brother. My sister-in-law, my brother's wife Shirley would not allow my niece April to join the family at the hospital to say good bye to my brother Richard her dying father one last time. I heard my sister Mary, my third oldest sister sneaked my niece April in the hospital behind my sister-in-law, Shirley back so she could say good bye to her dying father. All the family members were standing around, my brother Richard hospital bed because he was dying. Some family members decided to leave the hospital before my brother Richard died. My brother died on their way home. They had to turn around and come back to the Hospital. Myself, my son Reginald stayed in my brother's hospital room with his wife Shirley and their grandchildren. We decided to walk out my brother hospital room to sit outside his hospital room.

When I asked my brother Richard wife Shirley, if she could still hear my brother Richard breathing. My brother wife Shirley, ran back into my brother hospital room. My brother Richard was dead my brother Richard took his last breath when his wife Shirley, his grandchildren Aaron and Ebony, myself and my son Reginald step out his hospital room for just a few minutes. The hospital personnel or doctor came in my brother Richard hospital room and pronounce my brother Richard death. The doctor or hospital personnel ask my brother wife Shirley if she would donate my brother's Eyes, she said yes. My brother wife planned my brother's funeral. She left word with the funeral home that no one was allow to see my brother body without her consent. She did not want my brother daughter April to say her good byes at the hospital that night. When my brother Richard was dying. The day of my brother Richard funeral.

Shirley, my brother wife was still blocking my Brother Daughter April from viewing her father (daddy) body. Or attend his funeral. The day before my brother Richard funeral my daughter Kimberly called and told me her cousin April, my brother Richard daughter (my niece) was with her and that she did not understand because my brother wife Shirley would not let her spend time with her daddy. When he was sick, (she took medical when she was in College). His wife would not let her come to the hospital to say her good byes to her daddy (father). when he died that night in the hospital. All the family was able to say their good byes. The day of the funeral his wife Shirley was still blocking her from seeing or Saying her good byes to her father. My daughter Kimberly brought my brother Richard daughter April her cousin to my brother Richard funeral. My brother Richard Mitchell was married to his wife Shirley Mitchell for 40 years my brother Richard died in 2009 of lung cancer. Before my brother was diagnosed with cancer, he worked for a company named Mescon. This company installed home carpeting, home ceiling, and floor tile. He worked for this company for 10-15 years. Prior to him getting sick with cancer. I think my brother working with this company cause my brother cancer. Because my brother worked for this company for years installing panel type celling, replaceable type ceiling. It was found that this type ceiling has asbestos in it and causes cancer. My brother wife Shirley Mitchell was a School teacher she worked for school district for 20 years. My brother never had any kids by his wife Shirley but he adopted his wife Shirley 2 years old daughter. That my brother Richard raised as his own daughter. Her name was Bonnie(boo). Bonnie grew up and Had a daughter and a son through her marriage. after her marriage ended. My brother Richard and his wife Shirley daughter Bonnie(Boo) after, six or seven years moved away to another City and state. My brother Richard and his wife Shirley took custody of there grandchildren and adopted their grandchildren after a certain amount of years. The grand son was about 13 years old and the Granddaughter was about 16 years old. In 2009 when my brother Richard died. In 2012 my brother Richard wife Shirley had a stroke. In the year 2016, my brother Richard wife Shirley died. My brother Richard was born with a Knot on the very top of his head. My brother Richard lived with that knot on the top of his head from birth. He had surgery at age 18 years old. But from birth to age 18 when my brother Richard had his surgery, my brother Richard lived with that knot on his head it was putting pressure on his brain and keeping him from learning. He was passed by his teachers each year all the way up to 12th grade and he could not learn or read. All the siblings in the family teased one another and my brother Richard grew up with his sisters and brothers in the family teasing him and calling him nipple knotty (his nick name) Because he was born with that knot on the top of his head. Because my brother Richard and his wife Shirley was married for forty years and his wife was a school teacher and a school counselor for 20 years. She taught him how to read and write. Over the years. Plus, he had a daughter, grandson, and granddaughter, to work with him academically. My brother love getting dressed up and going to the club and drinking and coming home 3-4 in the Morning. I always said that my brothers could not be my man if they were not my brothers and I Never understand how their wife put up with them as husbands because all of my brother Were married for 30-40 years. Before they died. My sister-in-law Shirley like going To bingo and gabling but her and my brother spent time with their family and went to church on Sundays.

My sister Bernadette Mitchell Squire Jones my fourth younger sister grew up in the family home, Attended the Immaculate Conception Catholic School, Charleston, South Carolina. Along with All the siblings in the Mitchell family of John and Christabell Mitchell, In Charleston, South Carolina. She graduated a Vocational High School in Long Island, New York. Where she lived with My Oldest brother William, his wife and kids. When my sister Bernadette returned home to Charleston, South Carolina after her High School Graduation in Long Island, New York. My sister Bernadette had this new saying while she sat at the dinner table after she ate. She would yell out "Umm boy that was good" everyone at the dinner table would just look at her. Like my other sisters and brothers my sister Bernadette had the Mitchell family trade mark. she knew How to make the people in her presence laugh so hard. "she is the life of the party, "no fool no fun." My sister Bernadette Mitchell

Squire Jones were married twice she have two children Robert and Adrienne Squire. She married her Kids father the marriage lasted 10 years. She fell in love twice after her divorce but she finally met her second husband, Major Jones they married. He was in the Air force, He was stationed on the Charleston, South Carolina Air Force Base. He was married prior to his marriage with my sister Bernadette to a white woman. He had two grown kids a son and a daughter by his first wife where he lived and was stationed in Alaska. His kids were bi-racial. My fourth oldest sister Bernadette and her husband Major Jones eventually, invested in a home. They bought the family home from my baby brother Andrew timothy Mitchell. They adopted my niece son Harry, my sister Bernadette worked at Charleston County Library, Charleston, South Carolina For years while she was married. My sister Bernadette divorce her husband Major Jones after 11 years. When my sister Bernadette met and married her husband Major he was in the military. My sister Husband military personnel, when he was in the military ordered him to attend substance abuse counseling but after my sister and her husband married and he was discharged from the Military, he discontinued his substance abuse counseling. My sister and her Husband had a dog Called nick. My sister husband would not go to work and drink all day. One day my sister car insurance was cancelled. Her husband got drunk one day and ask nick the Dog, should he tell my sister Bernadette that her car insurance was cancelled. My sister Bernadette husband moved out and move in with a girlfriend. The family house my sister Bernadette and her husband bought from my baby brother Andrew Mitchell was, located in the historic area of downtown Charleston, South Carolina. Therefore, the family House was considered a historic home. My sister Bernadette divorced her husband. My sister had a problem with a young drug pusher hiding drugs in her yard. She argued with the young drug pusher (a young Blackman). He came back and shot my sister Bernadette home up while she was in her bedroom Upstairs. My sister was lucky because she had just got out of her bed to use the bathroom. If my sister was still lying down in her bed instead of getting up to use the bathroom, those bullets shot into her Home would have killed her and she would not be living today.

After, my sister Bernadette house (home) was shot up by the drug pusher. Bullets, my sister Bernadette Placed her home (house) up for sale for $130.000 dollar because it was historic. But she made a mistake of Taking out a loan on her home (house) to renovate the home (house) but she could not pay the loan Back. So the bank foreclosed on the family home. And my sister lost the family home that was in the Family for decades. My sister lost the family house. She moved in with her daughter Adrienne. After my sister lost her house she retired her job at the county library, Charleston, South Carolina. My sister health began to fail after losing her home and her job at the same time. It took a toll on My sister Bernadette.

My sister Louise Mitchell Simmons is the third younger sister. Louise attended the Immaculate Conception Catholic School in Charleston, South Carolina. And Bishop England High catholic school Charleston, South Carolina. She like all of Christabell and John Mitchell children that grew up in the family home on the historic downtown area of Charleston, South Carolina. She was also of the catholic religion and belong to Our Lady of Mercy catholic church. As did the entire Mitchell family Children. Louise married her husband Robert Simmons they have four children, Robert Jr. Rodney, Leslie, and Toni Lynn Anne Simmons. My sister Louise and her husband live in apartments during the Early years of their marriage. My sister Louise and her husband began to invest in Real Estate. My sister Louise and her husband Initially bought their family home. My sister Louise and her husband invested in other rental property. My sister Louise and her husband over the years invested in three homes. That they rented to Tenants For profit. They also owned and operated a nursing home. (Residential home). My sister Louise and her Husband Robert has been married for 40 years. My sister Louise and her husband, kids and grandkids are grown. My sister and her husband is up in age. My sister and her husband recently lost a grandson that that they practically raised. The grandson was age 14. He died from asthma

My sister Louise also had a sense of humor and the ability to make the people in her presence Laugh. This was an ability that all my family siblings (sisters and brothers) had and still have Today. The ability to make people around them laugh is a hereditary strait that Christabell And John Mitchell children inherited because our mother had a sense of humor and the ability To make people around her laugh. I think out of all the Mitchell children I was the only quiet sibling in the family. I was an introvert growing up, Now you can't shut me up. My sister Louise and her husband has done an excellent Job raising their kids and grandkids. My sister and her husband has largely contributed to there Children and grandchildren success in life. My sister and her husband Robert spent a great deal of their life operating and running there Nursing home (Residential home) and taking care of their nursing home tenants. They finally retired and close down their residential home and went out of business.

My baby brother Andrew timothy Mitchell was born with a very bad stutter speech problem. When my brother was a little boy he loved playing with this green electric football game with his Friends. Family siblings laugh and joke about him and his friends playing with green military army men with riffles in their hands moving them around on a football field instead of football players. I don't remember why he did not have football players instead of army men with riffles I remember when my baby brother Andrew was about 3 or 4 years old, cute with a light complexion. He had these two big cheeks and he stutter when he spoke, it was hard for him to get his words out. Family and friends, would play with my baby brother because he was so cute. They would have him say his name. He would say, my name is Andrew timothy Mitchell, they would say to him, "now do that thing," then he would do this cute little dance and they would give him money for doing the dance and saying his name. My brother Andrew Attended Immaculate Conception Catholic School, Charleston, South Carolina. And he graduated from Charles A. Brown High School, Charleston, South Carolina. After my brother, completed high School he fell in love and married his high school sweet Brenda. My brother Andrew join the Military. My brother Andrew and his wife was stationed as military Personnel in Atlanta, Georgia. My brother and his wife had three children, one daughter tiffany, Two sons Ashley and Andrew timothy Jr. Mitchell.

My brother Andrew served twenty years in the United States Army, US Military. He retired in 1995. When my brother retired out the Military, he was unable to find a job. I would drive him around to look for a job for months. He finally left, Charleston, South Carolina and moved to Columbia, South Carolina. He found a job and an apartment. He met and fell in love with a young lady that he later married. This was his second marriage. Her family was from the family home town of Charleston, South Carolina. He was so much in love it Broke his heart when his marriage failed for the second time around. This was a second failed marriage. He pledged he would never marry again. He attended and graduated college As an Optometrist. He Attempted to work in Optometry but decided he wanted to work in sales instead. He started a self-employed business. He began to sell beauty supplies. He began to sell products that He developed himself. He began to establish his business going long distance. He would use his car For his business. He used his own personal vehicle and he drove city to city, state to state. To beauty Shops, and barber shops selling his beauty supplies. He established a very successful business. He met His third wife. They moved from Columbia, South Carolina to Atlanta, Georgia My brother Andrew and His wife Ann partnered together selling beauty supplies. They bought their first home. A beautiful Home that they bought in Atlanta, Georgia. My brother and his wife team up as husband and wife in Their self—employed beauty supplies business. My brother and his wife partnership business became Very profitable. They were in business for at least 15 years. My brother clientele grew and kept him And his wife on the road. My brother Andrew and his wife Anne became traveling sales persons. Where they were constantly traveling. Their clients were in the hundreds. I attended Barber styling College in Goose Creek, South Carolina. My brother Andrew would travel from Atlanta, Georgia to the Family home town of Charleston, South Carolina. Selling his products (beauty supplies). My old barber College instructor, and my brother Andrew became close friends. My brother still sells his Products, beauty supplies to my old instructor Mr. Howard today. My brother and his wife rented the beautiful family home they bought in Atlanta, Georgia. Because their business was so successful they decided to rent the first home. They bought in Atlanta, Georgia. And decided to rent the first home out to tenants and they invested in a second beautiful home in Atlanta,

Georgia. They lived in Atlanta, Georgia for 15 to 20 years. My brother and his wife decided to move from Atlanta, Georgia about 2012. To the family home town of Charleston, South Carolina. They decide To build a beautiful home in Charleston, South Carolina. Where my brother lived and grew up. As of 2016 my brother and his wife live in a big home that they built from the ground up. They are renting the homes they bought in Atlanta, Georgia. My brother and his wife has retired. Their beauty supplies business I have not seen my brother newly built home but heard his home is Like a mansion and beautiful. I have not seen my brother in 4 years.

My sister Sylvia is the fourth oldest sister out of 8 girls and 8 boys in the Mitchell family, in the family Home town of Charleston, South Carolina. Like all the children of John and Christabell Mitchell Sylvia Mitchell Myers Scott knows how to make the people around her laugh is a Mitchell family trait. My sister Sylvia like all my other older siblings helped with the younger siblings in the family. Especially, after daddy died in 1960 and left my mama with fourteen children to raise. Although, my mama was a strong black woman. My sister Sylvia is the last oldest living sibling and the oldest decision maker of the Mitchell family. From 2000 to present 2017 the family has suffered, tremendous lost life of family members both from Younger to oldest. The family suffered a significant lost in 2011, when my sister Mary died She was the oldest family sibling that all the family members looked up to whenever there was a Family crisis. Especially, after mama died in 1989. After the family buried my sister Mary in 2011 The remaining 5 siblings Joke about who was going to take my sister Mary place as being that family member that the family can turn to during family crisis. My sister Sylvia is the oldest sibling left (living). The family have 5 remaining siblings left out of Christabell and John Mitchell 16 children. The siblings left are the four youngest siblings:

My baby brother, Andrew timothy Mitchell, myself Lavern A Lincoln, The third youngest, the fourth Youngest Louise Simmons, The Fifth younger Bernadette Jones, The family last oldest sibling Sylvia Scott. After my sister Mary funeral in 2011, the last remaining 5 siblings sat around my sister Mary's 2 story home downstairs dining area discussing, who was going to take my sister Mary place in the Family. Who was going to take charge in time of family crisis. No one volunteered but my sister Sylvia Is the last living oldest child of John and Christabell Mitchell. My sister Sylvia has been married several times her first marriage was When she was 15 like my parents. She was young and very impressionable. She fell In love with the first Young man she dated. She got pregnant at age 15 years old. My mama did not believe in pregnancy And not being married. My sister got pregnant in 1950, 1960, when pregnancy out of wedlock was Frowned upon by our parents and the public. This was also during a period in time if you Were under age your parents had to sign for there under age children to get married. My mama signed for My sister Sylvia to get married. She was under age and pregnant but my sister ended up Marrying a Husband who stayed in trouble with the law. My sister had five children for her husband 4 daughters And 1 son. My sister was in love very impressable. But eventually, my sister realized she loved her Husband and the father of her five children but she did not have a husband and her children did not Have a father because he stayed in trouble with the law, Her husband stayed in jail the entire marriage. My sister was young and in love with her husband. My sister Sylvia were so in love with her husband that she would visit her husband while he was in Jail. During her marriage. The story in the family goes that my sister Sylvia conceive at least two of her children in jail. My sister was still young She married at age 15. She was married with children but she still wanted to party with her friends And sisters. She liked going out to the night club and party. My mama being the strong black woman That she was giving birth to 16 children herself at a young age when she got married to my father Took control, and allowed my sister Sylvia and her children to live with the family and the family was there for my sister Sylvia and her five children, my sister seek government assistance. My sister Sylvia and my sister Mary married as teenagers. at the young age of 15 and 16 years old. Because they got pregnant. They never had a marriage and their children never had a father because Their husband was in jail more than they were out of jail. They were young and could not stop Broking the law. My sister Zenobia was a teenager when she married her husband. She was not Pregnant but she got married one day and her husband went to jail the next day. She never had a Marriage. My sisters Sylvia, Mary, and Zenobia never really had a marriage. They fell in love with The wrong men at a young age. My sisters Sylvia and Mary moved away as married teen moms. My teenage sisters moved to New York to work as live in maids, in order to take care of their children for about a year. The younger siblings and my mama took care of their children. My sister Sylvia got Back with her husband. My sister Sylvia, her husband and the children moved to Baltimore, Maryland For several years. My sister Sylvia eventually moved back home with her children to live back with the Family and to the family home town of Charleston, South Carolina. My family has always been there for my sister Sylvia and her children. My sister Sylvia eventually, got her own apartment and moved out And applied for government assistant for her and her children. My sister Sylvia as the years pasted, met Her younger children father, his name was Kenneth Scott. He was married. He Installed wall to wall carpeting, He worked with my sister Mary male friend, Allen. Allen and Scott Worked in the same profession, installing residential and commercial wall to wall carpeting. Both my sisters, Mary and Sylvia finally met professional hard working men in their lives. Both my sisters, Mary and Sylvia men eventually own and operated their own self employed Business installing residential and commercial carpeting. My sister Sylvia gave birth to her second Child for Kenneth Scott. He was married. My sister Sylvia got pregnant with a second child for Scott. While my sister Sylvia was pregnant with Scott second child. She gave him an Ultimatum, she told him if he did not leave her apartment. Go home pack his clothes, leave his wife and children and move in with her and his expected child. Or don't come back to her house any more. He went home and pack his clothes and left his wife and children. They lived together. She had his son. She already had his daughter, he was Self-employed. They got married and bought a home. They were married a total of 10 years. She helped him with his Carpet Installation business. She took care of his payroll for years, while they were married. she attended cosmetology college, graduated and opened her own beauty salon.

She owned and operated her own beauty salon for 15 years. She turned the business over to her daughter, who is also a cosmetologist. She opened another business in the historic area of downtown, Charleston, South Carolina. Only blocks away from where the family grew up and where the family home was located. She rented a table in the old slave market an historic landmark. She wrote two children books that she sold at her table in the market and she invented and obtained a patten for the items that she also sold at her table in the Market. In the historic area of downtown Charleston, South Carolina. She still owns and operate this business today 2017. She still lives in the home her husband Scott bought for the family, Her Husband Scott died in 2000.

My family owned two houses on the eastside of the City of Charleston, South Carolina. The houses were 2 story houses. The houses both had an upstairs and a downstairs. My parents always rented one house to tenants The upstairs was rented to one family and the downstairs was rented to a second family. The Second house was the family home. The family home had an upstairs and a downstairs. The upstairs were the bedrooms of the 14 remaining (the first two children died at a young age) children in the family and my parent bedrooms. Downstairs of the family home was the dining room, living room, the kitchen and the hallway. The kitchen was in the back down stairs area of the family home with a kitchen door that lead to The family backyard. The backyard was full of large trees especially a tree that was called the weeping Willow tree. The children in the family would play and swing on this weeping willow tree. My older sister Hermine would threaten to whip us (children) if we did not stop swinging on this tree.

My Parents were self-employed they sold the lumber wood for the pot belly stove that families used back in the 30s, 40s, 50s, 60s. My family was middle class catholic family. My parents had a total of 16 Children. 8 boys and 8 girls. The first 2 boys died at a very young age. My parent was John and Christabell Mitchell. My family did not really have money problems until my father died in 1960. And my mama had to raise fourteen children as single parent. When my father died money was tight in the family especially after my mama attempted to seek assistance from state welfare department and was told she would have to sell the family two houses, to be eligible for state welfare assistance.

My mama began to work and my older sisters and brothers (siblings) dropped out of school, join the military worked at the corner grocery store did their part to be of assistance and help mama to take care of the family after daddy died. I could remember as a child having to eat sugar bread, tea and bread, the family had a waffle making machine my mama would mix the waffle batter and pour the waffle batter inside the waffles making machine and close the top part of the waffle machine down on the waffle batter to make the waffle. My mama made waffle and pancakes a lot for the family breakfast.

I still remember the Aunt Jemima pancake mix and Aunt Jemima syrup my mama mix and cook for the family Breakfast. I ate cereal so much as a child I turned against it. I remember there was a neighborhood shoe store around the corner from the family home. I remember mama would buy $3.00 and $5.00 shoes for myself and my sisters and brothers (siblings) to wear. My mama also work at the catholic church (Our Lady of Mercy) 2 street blocks down the family home. The church would give my mama clothes for the children in the family. The fourteen children in the family attended the Immaculate Conception Catholic school free of charge because my family was catholic. I remember Standing up in the school yard at Immaculate Conception Catholic School and my 1st grade teacher During lunch period (sister Jean Marie) walked up to me gave me lunch told me that my aunt told Her to give me lunch. She gave me lunch on more than one occasion.

My mama eventually opened up a sweet shop in the front downstairs area of the family home. She sold groceries, she bought a juke box, which was a big record player for her clients to put quarters in and play their favorite latest records. My mama would put a quarter in the juke box and play the record she liked by Diana Ross and she would just start snapping her finger and dancing and singing. Just having fun all by herself. My mama also sold beer for her customers inside the sweet shop. She also had other small Business that gave her income to help support the family. My mama work as a maid at a Baptist church. And I heard from my older siblings that mama and daddy bought the family home from this white Lady she worked for as a maid I think this happen before daddy died. I believe the white lady that Sold my mama and daddy the family home, sold my parents the family home during the time white people was moving out the area my family live in because the blacks were moving in. The white people was moving out because they did not want to live around the blacks. Now as of 2017 the white people is moving back in the family neighborhood because my family homes and other homes in the family neighborhood is in the historic area of the city of Charleston, South Carolina and worth a lot of money. My family home is historic. But my sister Bernadette lost the family home. She was going to sell the family home for $130,000 but took a bank loan out on the family home attempting to renovate family home before selling it for 130,000. she could not pay the loan back the bank foreclosed and she lost family home before she made the sale of $130,000. I heard my mama worked. as a maid and baby sat for this wealthy white lady on the battery a historic area of Charleston, South Carolina White lady down on the battery the historic area of Charleston, South. It was a struggle when my daddy died but thank god my mama was a strong black Woman. My mama is my role model to this day.

My parents had 8 boys and 8 girls, I was the third younger Child. I had a younger sister and a younger brother. The first two boys my parents had, died at a very young age. I had 5 older brothers and 6 older sisters. My older sisters and brothers did the household chores. My parents own the family house. The children in the family did the wallpapering and painting of the walls and interior of the family house. As one of the younger siblings I remember painting and wall papering the interior of the family house with my older siblings. I help with cleaning the family house(home), as I got older. My brothers helped my parents with their lumber wood, self-employed business and painting of the family home. My older sisters helped with the younger siblings (children)they help my mama with the cooking and cleaning.

My mama would cook a big meal every Sunday. The family would attend the catholic church 2 street Blocks down from the family home, (Our Lady of Mercy Catholic Church). After, Sunday Mass(Church) My mama would prepare a large Sunday meal for the family. My mama would cook a big pot of collars Greens or turnip green, fried chicken, macaroni and cheese, potato salad, bake sweet potato, In the oven, candy jams with sweet potato, bake corn bread, sweet potato pie or apple pie. My mama would sometimes prepare red rice, and chicken or pork chop, corn on the cobb, or can Corn, or can sweet peas, or can string beans, or I love it when she prepares a big pot of fresh Snap beans with fresh neck bone and white potatoes white rice with. I still love the pork and beans and rice. My mama would cook waffles with syrup, pancakes with syrup Grits with scramble eggs and pork sausage, or bacon. As one of the children in the Mitchell family I ate so much cereal with milk that I turned against milk and cereal as I got older, my mom own a waffle and pancake maker machine The old fashion, way of preparing pancake You had to mix eggs, milk, and water to the pancake mix Today 2017, you buy store bought Pancake mix complete in the box. All the ingredient has been added In the box for you. The old fashion, way of mixing pancakes with eggs, milk and water was also use To prepare waffles, you just poured the mix in the waffle machine. As a younger sibling, I learned how To cook by watching my mama and my older sisters. (siblings) My mama and my older sisters taught me to cook as I got older. As I became an adult with my own family. I still love to prepare certain soul foods or traditional meals. That was cooked or prepared as I grew up. I especially, still like family traditional Sunday meals such as: Collard greens, and rice, macaroni and cheese, potato salad, candy jams, swee Potato pie, bake corn bread, red rice and chicken, pork and beans and rice and pork chop, lima bean And rice with hot sauce. My favorite traditional meal especially during holidays, Christmas an Thanksgiving is Turkey, collard greens, and rice, Potato salad with a little mustard in it, macaroni and cheese extra cheese, 2 sweet potato pie or candy jams. I love a can cranberry sauce on the side. For New Year Day dinner I would fried chicken or barbecue some chicken, 2 sweet potato pies Or bake a pan of candy jams, potato salad with a little mustard and a pan of macaroni and cheese extra cheese.

My family attended Our Lady of Mercy church religiously every Sunday. After Church (mass) the family ate a big meal together, prepared by my mama and my sisters. My family would drive as a family, every Sunday after church to visit family members, that lived on an island called johns island, South Carolina. My family lived downtown, historic area of the city of Charleston, South Carolina. My family had a total of 16 children 8 boys and 8 girls, the first two boys died at a very young age. Because there were so many children in the family, my parents bought all the children in the family a Pair of skates for Christmas. All the Children in the family,

39

younger and older would skate On the neighborhood streets the family home was located and in the immediate area where the family lived. The children in the family, would skate as a family every year on Christmas day. All the children in my family neighborhood would be in the middle of the neighborhood streets Skating on Christmas day and after Christmas.

My mama would take the children in my family to the County Fair, every year when the County fair Came to town. I could still remember my mama putting the children in my family coats on because Every year in Charleston, South Carolina where the family lived, the weather did not change to cold weather or winter weather until the County Fair came to town. Today 2017, The county Fair still come to South Carolina the same time of the year the end of October to the beginning of November. This is a Tradition everyone that lives in South Carolina knows that when the County Fair come to town In Ladson, South Carolina Its time to take out their heavy winter coats. Especially, if you are going to attend County Fair. The County Fairgrounds is always cold every year. You know to take out your heavy coats.

During Thanksgiving and Christmas the family normally enjoyed a family gathering after a big meal. A Turkey, potato salad, Macaroni and cheese, collard greens, or turnip greens apple pie, sweet potato Pie candy jams, baked sweet potato. The family children normally, enjoyed Christmas with the other Children in the neighborhood, skating, or whatever the neighborhood activities. The family normally Have the regular family gathering, enjoying the family time together on Christmas day. My siblings were Always full of fun, lots of jokes, teasing one another and on the floor laughing at each sibling clowning Around, laughing so hard they had tears in their eyes. All the family siblings knew how to make everyone laugh and have fun. Holiday, Christmas, Thanksgiving was always lots of fun, when My family got together. The family member that has left this life is dearly missed every day.

Birthday in my family was celebrated together because there were so many children in my Family. For Example, my birthday is March 21, 1951 and My sister Bernadette birthday is March 22. 1949 My sister

Bernadette and I was 3 years apart but people would actually, take me for my sister Bernadette and took my sister Bernadette for me. I did not think we looked that much a like People could not tell myself and my sister Bernadette apart. This almost got me beaten up because This boy took me and my sister Bernadette for one another. My sister Bernadette and my birthday Were right after the other so our Birthday was celebrated together.

B) <u>My Community I Grew Up In</u>

I grew up in a lower income area in 1950s, 1960s, 1970s on the eastside of Charleston, South Carolina. My parents moved in this area of town. The white race was moving out and blacks were moving In the neighborhood. The white race did not want to live around the blacks. This was a period when racism existed. A time during segregation. My mama bought the family home from this white lady, She worked for as a maid. I could remember my mama taking the Children in the family to Martin Luther King Jr. march during the 1950s, 1960s. This was a time when blacks were fighting for equal rights, civil rights, And equal pay. The neighborhood was segregated. The area the family lived and grew up was violent. if you were disrespectful, your neighbors disciplined you. Growing up you were taught to say yes mam and no mam and you were discipline by your parents if you did not respect your elder. My mama whipped us with the electric cord but she would also throw the first thing she got in her hands at us if we try to run Away from her, when she was disciplining us. I remember one day, I was upstairs in the family home.

The family home was 2 stories. I was upstairs in my family home. My mama was trying to Discipline me, I try to run down the family home stairway to get away. My mama would throw Something at us if we try to get away. Back during this period, parents use what they call a Metal tin tub to wash clothes in. I attempted to run away and my mama help me down The stairs. She threw the little metal tub behind me, it helped me down the stairs. Because it hit me from behind While I was running down the family home stairs. The family home stairway was outside The family home. The stairway extended from the upstairs porch to the down stairs porch.

Growing up In the 50s, 60s families in my neighborhood left their doors open at night and all day. They also left their windows open. There was no threat of violence or home invasion. There were fights in the neighborhood and I also heard of gangs but disrespect was not allowed by our parents. Parents Disciplined you for being disrespectful especially to your elders. Families sat on the porch in their bras Because of the heat and no air condition. Electric fans and the cool air and breeze were the only means of cooling off from the heated days and nights. Air condition was not invented yet.

The neighborhood was low income. I grew up in the 1950s, 1960s, 1970s in the city of Charleston, South Carolina. My parents owned 2 two stories homes, upstairs and downstairs. All the houses in my neighborhood were 2 stories houses, upstairs and downstairs. The neighborhood Had small grocery stores that sold groceries and was also a meat market. You could walk one street block or ½ street block to the grocery store morning to closing at night, the owners of the grocery store placed their close sign on the door or store window that the store was closed that night. There were neighborhood churches on the corner a street block or 2 street block from your home Within walking distance from your home. My family attended a catholic church about 2 street blocks away from the family home. There were 16 children in my family the first 2 boys died at a very young age. My parents, (Christabell and John Mitchell). My parents walked all 16 children (siblings) 8 boys 8 girls 2 street blocks from the family home every Sunday religiously. All the grocery stores, churches, Playgrounds, were within walking distance from neighborhood family home. There also were public Transportation. The city bus. That would take families in the neighborhood to the grocery stores, Churches, schools, playground etc. that was not within street block walking distance. The Fare or cost for the Bus, Public Transportation was 10 cents or 15 cents.

The neighborhood Shopping Area where the families in the neighborhood shopped for clothes, shoes, home accessories, furniture, Anything for families in the neighborhood homes or children and families were about 5 street blocks Or you were able to pay 10 cents or 15 cents to ride on the public transportation, (the city bus). Clothes, shoes, items for the homes were within walking distance and the cost was cheap. The cost Of living were cheap. The families did not make a lot of money. Parents only made a couple of dollars an hour. During the summer when it was hot parents and families would sit on the porch, sleep with Their door and window up or open. You could walk past a home or apartment and you would see an elderly person sitting on their porch With the doors open or window up during the daytime. Or at night. because it was too hot to stay inside Your home or apartment. The only way to stay cool from the heat in 50s, 60s, was an electric fan That our parents sat on the floor or in their window during the day or at night with the door and window open to stay cool. Some parents would sit on the porch during the day or night time in their bra and no other top. Back in the time I grew up the children in the neighborhood respected their elders.

There were fights in the neighborhood and there were talk of gangs but other than occasional fights In the neighborhood. When the city police or law enforcement were called and the person or persons Were taken to jail. But respect especially respect for your elder was the rule when I was growing up. If you were disrespectful to your teacher, parents, your elders, your parents discipline you with their hands Or you got a whipping with a belt or electric cord. Children in the 1950s, 1960s, 1970s were taught to Say yes mam and no mam if you did not have the respect that your parents taught you as a child you got A whipping. Or disciplinary actions by your parents. But you were disciplined or punished. Now days You cannot discipline children or kids with a belt or electric cord. Now days you can go to jail for child Abuse or your children is taken away from you by child protective services.

The major merchant (shopping) and Business area was located, in the City of Charleston, South Carolina. Downtown Charleston, street blocks away from the family neighborhood. The major businesses, Furniture stores, clothing stores, shoe stores, department stores, all major stores and businesses was Located on King street the major Shopping and business area in the city of Charleston, South Carolina. King Street from the family home was 4 street blocks and within walking distance. The shopping area That was not within the city street blocks and walking distance were accessible by riding on the city Of Charleston, South Carolina transportation, city bus for a cost of 10 cents or 15 cents fare. Prior to Desegregation anyone of the blacks or negro race had to sit on the back of the city bus or Transportation.

As a child growing up in the 1950s, 1960s and 1970s I remember my mama putting myself and my other siblings over coats on because the county fair was in the family home town of Charleston, neighboring town of Ladson, South Carolina the largest Town or city I remember visiting when I was young. My mama Christabell Mitchell always put the children in the family coats on when the coastal Carolina fair came to town because the entire state of South Carolina knows that whenever the county fair comes to Ladson, South Carolina it's the winter season and it is time to take the winter clothes and coats out if you are going to attend the coastal Carolina fairgrounds in Ladson, South Carolina the largest city I remember going to when I was a young child. The Coastal Carolina Fair is an annual fair that occurs at the Exchange Park Fairground in Ladson, South Carolina. It lasts 11 days beginning on the last Thursday in October with music performance each night also, the fair has variety fair rides.

There are annual exhibits in creative arts, two flower shows, five arts and photography exhibits and farm Animals in both the agricultural and commercial buildings and a food fair. The Coastal Carolina is an all Volunteer fundraiser of exchange club of Charleston. The fair normally begins October 26, to November 5,[th]. Tickets are purchased through October 26 admission for adult and child according to age. The type of events are concerts, craft shows, animals show, and festivals. Coastal Carolina Fair, all fun Since 1957. The Exchange Park Fairground 9850 highway 78 Ladson, South Carolina has held successful Fair events at the Coastal Carolina Fair since 1957. The Exchange Park has been the ideal location To host events since 1957 with variety options, The Exchange Park Fairground offers many different Locations on the property that can be used for a variety of events. The Exchange Park is a great place for you to host, sales and trade show and livestock events. Large Group and community functions. Automobile, Motorcycle and RV assemblies. Concerts, and festivals The Exchange Park offers several buildings for rent with versatile space with these festivals. Great rented rates, free parking for your patrons, conveniently located at the crossroads of Charleston, Berkeley, and Dorchester counties. Large indoor outdoor facilities which offer countless options for all Types of events

C) Early Schooling

My family was catholic my family name was Mitchell my parents were John and Christabell. Growing up my family were a large family. Our parents own two homes they rented one home Out to tenants. The second was the family home. The family attended Our Lady of Mercy Catholic Church two streets blocks from the family home. The kids in the family attended Immaculate Conception Catholic School, Charleston, South Carolina. My parents had 16 kids and all 14 of the Living kids attended Immaculate Conception Catholic School. My parents could not afford to pay For 14 kids to attend Catholic School a private school but because my family was of the catholic Faith the family was allowed to attend Immaculate Conception free of charge. Out of 16 kids 14

Living kids attended Immaculate Conception Catholic School. I was the third youngest kid in the family. Immaculate Conception Catholic School was a School of middle class families. Most of the families were light complexion. Looking back, I think my family was the only family That could not afford to pay the school tuition. Most of the families that attended Immaculate Conception Catholic Private School the families were financially capable. My parents were middle Class family. My parents were self—employed selling lumber would for the pot belly wood stove used To heat families home during that time period in the 1940s through the 1950s. After daddy died in 1960 when I was 9 years old the family began to struggle because my mama was left with 14 children To raise. The help she had was my older sisters and brothers. After daddy died it was hard financially For my mom. My older brothers drop out Immaculate Conception Catholic School to work or Went in the military to help my mama after daddy died in 1960. The families that attended Immaculate Conception Catholic School were referred to by their last name. The kids in my family were referred To as the Mitchells. I remember other student family names like the

45

Thompsons, the Holmes The Holsters, the Pinckney family. etc. Sometimes I ran into students that attended the Immaculate Conception Catholic School that were in my brother Richard class or my sister Louise class, My sister Bernadette class, my sister Mary class, my sister Sylvia class, or my brother Gerald class If I ran into one of my sibling classmate they would all refer to me as one of the Mitchell. My parents paid for my sisters, brothers and myself to attend Immaculate conception catholic School when daddy was living but after daddy died Immaculate Conception catholic school continued to allow the kids in my family to continue attending Immaculate Conception Catholic School because it was a Catholic School.

I love attending a school of my religious faith, I love attending a school that my sisters and brothers attended. I did not like having to wear a school uniform. Public school kids wore regular Clothes to school every day back in the 1950s through the 1980s. I was an introvert as a child. I was So quiet I did not have any friends. I was quiet and did not speak to people. Though I was unfriendly I was such an introvert at school lunch period I stood up in the school yard by myself all through school. I hated when the teacher called on me to ask a question or answer a class question. I remember standing up in the school yard doing lunch period and my 1st grade teacher brought me Lunch. She told me my aunt brought the lunch to the school and told her to give it to me. My family Struggle because my family was a large family. Especially when my father died. Part of attending catholic School a private school was the students attended mass(church) once or twice a week all the kids in the various classes pre-school all the way to 12th grade lined up according to classroom and walk from the classroom to the school church on the school grounds. As a young child attending school and being An introvert and no friends and had to stand up in the school yard every lunch period by myself because I did not have any friends to hang out with doing lunch period. I never went to any of the school games or functions because I was so quiet and such an introvert. My family picked on me because I was the Quietest of all my siblings. I was also picked on by kids in the neighborhood because I was the quietest Of all my siblings. One night I walked to the neighborhood restaurant to buy some chicken box for myself and my siblings on my way back to my house I was walking through a neighborhood park on my way back home I was 18 years old and I was pregnant with my son but my mama did not know because I was afraid to tell my mama. and I was attacked by 6 neighborhood teenage kids simply because I was the quietest sibling out all my sisters.

The only time I participated in games during lunch period was when my baby sister Odessa, who was one year younger than I was. She was playing the game with me and our other classmate. I got left Back in first grade 2 times (I always told people as I was growing up that my teacher sister Jean Marie My 1ˢᵗ grade teacher. The teacher that brought me lunch every day and told me my aunt brought me the Lunch as I was standing up in the school yard by myself at lunch period. I always made a joke that sister Jean Marie kept me back in first grade because she liked me. Which is how my baby sister Odessa caught up with me in the first grade and we ended up in the same class the same year at Immaculate Conception catholic school.) I would tell people that my 1ˢᵗ grade teacher kept me back in first grade Because she liked me. The nun name was sister Jean Marie. Because I got left back twice in first grade My baby sister Odessa caught up with me in school. We were in the same grade and the same class. So, We ended up playing together at lunch period. I got kept back in the third grade also, I had a nice teacher in the first grade she would bring me lunch. Whenever I stood up at lunch period in the school yard by myself sister Jean Marie would tell me one of my relative brought my lunch for me. I knew she was not telling me the truth even though I was in the first grade. I had a nice first grade teacher but I had a mean nun for a teacher in 8ᵗʰ grade. One day while I was in class, my 8ᵗʰ grade teacher sister Mary Francis my 8ᵗʰ grade teacher called me outside my classroom into the hallway and that nun hit my head up against the hall way wall outside my classroom. I believe sister Mary Francis was also Immaculate Conception catholic School principal back then during that period in my life time back in the 1950s Through the 1960s. I never told my mom that teacher hit my head up against the school wall that day. I could remember But never forgot the experience to this day. Some of the subjects I took as a student at Immaculate Conception catholic school was catholic religious courses as well as the regular academic courses. But Thinking back, I remember to this day that I actually learned more about my religious courses than I Learned about my academic courses. I hated going to class I hated going to school. All my sisters and brothers hated going to school at Immaculate Conception catholic school.

When it would rain on school days I would intentionally get wet up from the rain so I would have a Reason not to go to school that day. I would go back home wet from the rain my mama would whip me with the electric cord from the iron. My mama made me change into another school uniform and take Me to school no matter how late I was for school. I must have learned this behavior from my older sisters and brothers because my mama had to take my sisters and brothers back to school too Because they got wet in the rain on rainy school days also.

D) <u>Friends and Interest</u>

My spare time during my early age growing up was spent with my 13 sisters and brothers (siblings) on a Daily basis. My parents had 16 children, the first two boys died at a very young age, I was raised with 13 sisters and brothers. The siblings in the family was close, we went to school together at the Immaculate Conception Catholic School, Charleston, South within walking distance 8 Street blocks from the family Home. On Sunday, the family attended catholic church, Our Lady of Mercy religiously every Sunday 2 street block from the family home. The family ate together every day. The older sisters and brothers would gather with the Younger siblings and, the siblings would gather around in one of the room in the family home. The older Siblings would sometimes tell the younger siblings ghost stories. The Older sisters and brothers would take turn making jokes or teasing the younger siblings or other older Siblings Because my older siblings would tease and joke in a way that make everyone in the room laugh So hard they would be in tears and on the floor laughing. Family gathering for years were so much fun. Whenever the (siblings) sisters and brothers got together. Because there were so many siblings in the family, I don't think any of the sisters and brothers really Had any personal friends. The siblings in the family mostly spent time together. The sisters and Brothers were friends to one another. We fought as siblings I remember one day my sister Louise and I was fighting (I was the third youngest and she was the fourth youngest child out of 16 siblings she was 2 years older than me we were kid sisters fighting one another) my sister Louise fought dirty when you fought with her. We were fighting one day and she box me in my stomach I could not breath I told her to let me rest for a minute because I was out breath. My older sisters tease me about that for years. I could especially still in my mind hear my second oldest Sister Zenobia laughing at me with my other oldest siblings about me asking my sister Louise to stop fighting me and let me rest for a minute because she box me in my stomach and I could not breathe and I was out of breath. It was funny to me because my second oldest sister Zenobia, had such a hilarious, funny personality and everything came out her mouth was funny and she had such a Unbelievable laughable personality everything came out her mouth like my brother Gerald was funny. As the siblings got older they party together and hang out At my mama house and socialized together I was the quiet sibling in the family. I was an introvert. I mostly stayed to myself especially, in my younger age. I was so quiet that I was afraid to go to People I knew house, Afraid I did not know what to say. Whenever the (siblings) sisters and brothers Was having gatherings to have fun or to party, I was always in a corner by myself quiet. I was born with these two big pretty eyes. (my daddy had big eyes, all the girls in family had big eyes like our daddy). I would always get compliments on my eyes as I grew up. I was quiet but I would look People up and down without realizing that I was doing it. I was an introvert most of my young life growing up. My sister Zenobia gave me the nickname as a child of (Buckwheat like the black little boy in the 1950s and 1960s cartoon the little Rascals. I was given this name by my second oldest sister Zenobia because my mama had all these girls a total of 8 girls and she did not know how to do their hair so my mama would just braid the girls in the family hair in these three or four big braids like the little black boy on the cartoon the little rascals cartoon in the 1950s and 1960s and the fact that I had real big eyes like the little black boy on the cartoon The Little Rascal and the fact my skin was dark complexion did not help me. All the children in my family the Mitchell family looking back had nicknames the siblings in the family made up the nicknames my nickname was Buckwheat like the 1950s and 1960s cartoon character on the Little Rascals.

My mama had a sweet shop that she owned and operated on the front downstairs first floor of the Family home. My mama had a door installed where the customers would be able to enter the sweet shop area of the family home But I would work inside my mama sweet shop to help my mama with her sweet shop business. My mama had a best friend her name was Ms. Pearl, I became friend with Ms. Pearl daughter Patricia sometimes we would hang out together or go to a movie theatre. But I was quiet all my young Life. I did not get out of being an introvert or being quiet until I moved out my mama home and got My own apartment.

My favorite toy was skates. My parents would buy all the children in the family Skates for Christmas every year. I remember as a child myself and my sisters would make our own Doll baby from a glass soda bottle and we would use the grass white rope that was tied around the big block of ice that my Parents bought from the ice company that sold block ice. We would use the grass rope as the doll baby hair. We would use a soda bottle and we would open the grass white rope and secure it inside the glass soda bottle so we would be able to comb and style it as the doll baby hair. as I grew up in the 1950s and 1960s. We call it our grass doll baby.

Skates was the only toy my parents could afford every Year for Christmas I can still skate to this day. When my daughter was a teenager and I would take her And her friends to the skating ring I would also skate with them. I found it relaxing and fun, skating along With the music that was playing as I skated.

When I grew up the children was always asked what did they wanted to be when we grew up. I always Knew what I did not want to be. I knew I did not want to work in the medical field because I cannot Stand the site of blood. To this day 2017. I was interested in Modeling or acting. I am still interested to this day. I am a model but I have only invested but still have not made any money modeling.

My favorite movie to this day is the Christmas movie "Miracle on 34th street" a movie based on Santa Clause and Christmas in the 1950s. and another favorite movie was "Imitation of life." A movie base On 1930s, 1940s, and 1950s. Myself and my other younger sisters and brothers were only told ghost Stories I did not enjoy those ghost stories because I would wake in the middle of the night thinking I saw A ghost. The lights would be off in the middle of the night, I would be so afraid I would put my blanket over my head. And close my eyes real tight and try to go back to sleep. I don't remember having hobbies accept skating and playing with my grass doll baby that I made from a glass soda bottle and a grass roped that was tied around the block of ice bought by my parent from the ice company.

CHAPTER 2

Teenage Years

A) <u>Changes in my Family</u>

My relationship with my parents did not change when I became a teenager, my mama has always Been there for me all my life. I was quiet and very introverted into my teenage years. When I got into My teenage years about 12 years old because your mama or parents did not have the sex talk with There children when they got into puberty or teenage years, when I first saw my ministration cycle I Did not understand what was happening. I remember waking my mama up in the middle of the night To tell her that I was bleeding. She got up and just gave me a rag to use for my ministration period and A safety pin to use with the cloth or rag to keep it pinned to my panty. She still did not explain to me What was going on that I could remember. So. when I started seeing my first boyfriend at age 16 or 17 Years old when I started having sex I did not understand what I was doing. I was just having sex because That was what my boyfriend wanted to do. I was having sexual relations for a year before I got pregnant. When I got pregnant, I did not understand exactly what was going on. I knew I was pregnant, I tried Vinegar, doing exercise hoping I would lose my pregnancy because I was afraid to tell my mama, i was Pregnant. I finally told her when I was 8 months pregnant. I still would not agree to go to the doctor. My mama had to take my bed down before I would finally go to the doctor to be seen for my pregnancy. I went to the doctor one visit and I gave birth to my son. I was in labor for 12 hours before I finally gave Birth to my son. I believe he weighted, 6 pounds 11 ounces. I dropped out of school after I got pregnant And gave birth to my son. I had told the doctor that I had dropped out of school. When I went into Labor prior to giving birth to my son, I could hear the doctors down the hall from my hospital room Laughing saying that I was really having labor pains, I also could hear the doctor down the hall from My hospital room while I was in labor prior to me giving birth to my son. The doctor was saying that If I had stayed in school that I would have known to come to the doctor while I was pregnant. After, I gave birth to my son. My sisters and brothers, for years would tease and joke about My pregnancy. My brother Gerald really knew how to dose and tease you and have everybody on the floor laughing at you. For years, I had to endure my brother Gerald jokes about my pregnancy. During family gatherings and parties. I had to endure my brother Gerald joke about how I slept all day when I was pregnant with my son. How I grew a beard when I was pregnant, how mama had to take my bed down to make me go to the doctor when I was pregnant. For years, I was dose or teased by my sisters and brothers about my pregnancy. I was tease and dosed at family gatherings, at family parties.

My brother Gerald would have everybody on the floor laughing so hard at me for years. My other sister and brother dosed and teased me to for years. After I gave birth to my son at age 18 years old. My grandma daisy was staying with my family, She Had moved from Chicago, Illinois to Charleston, South Carolina. After—living away from the family for Years. She was a big help to me After I gave birth to my son. My mama was there for me like she has been there for me and my sisters and brothers all our lives. My mama has always been an independent Strong black woman when things goes wrong for me to the day she died in 1989. I remind myself that I Am my mama daughter to remind myself that my mama was a strong black woman because I am her Daughter I am strong just like my mama. Christabell Michell, my mama over the years, she taught All of her children to be survivors. To this day, myself and my siblings knows how to be strong and Survive whatever situation in life that may come our way.

My chores as a teenager were to help Clean the family home. Mop and make the beds in the family bedrooms, wash dishes, help with Wallpapering, or interior painting of the rooms in the family home. When I was growing up children could not talk back or be disrespectful with our parents if I was disrespectful my parents disciplined me. Children were not allowed to participate or be in grow up conversations or company. You were supposed to be as a child and make yourself invisible when in grown up company. I made the mistake one day as a younger sibling in the family. The family, was at the dinner table eating. The adults were in a conversation. it was my mama, my dad, my aunt, and a guest for dinner. I made the mistake of commenting in the adult conversation. My dad turned at the dinner table and slap me in my face so hard, I never got involved in my parent adult conversations again.

B) <u>School</u>

My favorite subject was Spelling and English, I loved the spelling bee test. It really helped my vocabulary.

My least favorite subject was math, I always hated math because I was never good at it. I attended Immaculate Conception Catholic School, Charleston, South Carolina, my most memorable teacher Was a (nun) sister Mary Frances in 8th grade. I believed she was also the principal at Immaculate Conception Catholic School when I attended. This was a private catholic school. The nuns were very Strict and they made sure the student learned and understood class courses. Sister Mary Frances were very strict but she wanted her students to be good students. I hated math all through school but When I was a student in sister Mary Frances class my math improved tremendously. I did not like sister Being so strict but I learned in her class. I appreciated the way she took time out with her students. Sister Mary Frances teaching technique help me to be a better student. The way she taught was a big Influence on my future academic with future classes I took. Immaculate Conception Catholic School Was a private school, all of the student girls, boys were smart students because the teachers(nuns) Took time with their students and made sure they learned. Immaculate Conception Catholic School, Was a private, Catholic School, the students were not categorized in groups but some students wereCatholic and some were not catholic.

I was perceived by others student as smart and I was real quiet and very introverted, I stayed to myself My baby sister Odessa was in my class. During recess, lunch Period my sister Odessa and I played kick ball with the other students at lunch period Immaculate Conception Catholic School had a basketball team but I was not on the school team. My plans were always to complete high school and attend college. I dropped out of high school and gave birth to my son. But my parents knew I wanted my education and that I wanted to return to high school and get my high school diploma. My intension was to complete college and my parents approved as parents, they always wanted better for their children. I only had one female friend as a teenager. As my friend, she wanted the best for me as I wanted the best for her in life. My friend as a teenager and later in my life. My friend also ended up pregnant as a teenager. but she also returned to high school after she had her son. She later got married and she gave birth to another son and a daughter. She also went to college. While she was married to her husband.

The boys and girls in my family as they got in their teens and older. They married gave birth to Their children. My oldest brother joined the military and move to Long Island, New York and started a family. My oldest sisters, Hermine and Zenobia moved to Albany, New York got married and started a family. My sister Hermine never returned to the family home town, Charleston, South Carolina except to visit or to attend, family funerals. My sister Zenobia return for visits and family funerals. She returned to the family home town of Charleston, South Carolina, after 20 years for about 4 years and return to Albany, New York, where she later died. But all of my sisters and brothers moved out my family home to start their lives. Some of my sisters and brothers settled down here in the family home town Charleston, South Carolina. Others moved away to New York and only returned for family visits and funerals.

C) Work

My mother owned her own sweet shop for years. My first job working was in my mama sweet shop. As a teenager. My next job as a teenager was after I gave birth to my son. I started working as a Waitress. My first waitress job was working at this drive through fast food restaurant. I also worked at Robertson Cafeteria Restaurant as a waitress. I worked at a Restaurant called Brooks Restaurant. I worked at the Mills Hyatt House Restaurant in the Mills Hyatt House Hotel as a waitress.

I did not contribute to my mother home or household. I still lived with my mother in her household but I just gave birth to my son and as a single mom I had to prove for my son. My mom never asked me for Part of my paycheck because she knew I had to provide for my son. My mom helped me with the care of my son. I asked if she wanted me to pay her. She told me to use my pay check to provide for myself and my son.

D) Social Life and Outside Interests

I was friends with my sisters and brothers (siblings). I had a friend her name was Patricia her mom Were my mom best friend. We went to the movies, we would hang out at her house when I visit Her house. I also began having male friends as a teenager at age 12 my husband that I married at age 21 years old was mostly at my house sitting outside my house on the porch or the stairway to my home. My parents were very strict about me dating or having a male (boyfriend in my teens). At age 15 my My mom would let me invite a male friend to my house but she would make her comments about him. I could only have my male friends at the house, only inside my home or stand on the porch or sitting on the Stairway. I began having male friends over to the house but I did not go on dates until I was abou 18 years old. I met my son father at age 18. He was about 20 years old. My mom allowed me to date when I met my son's father. He had his own apartment. He would pick me up at the family house. This was my first boyfriend (my son's father), his name was William. We would catch the bus after he got of Work. We would go to the movies and would go back to his apartment. My mom did not know he had his own apartment. We went on dates but we were not sleeping together, even though I went back to his apartment after our dates. After I started dating my son father at age 18, I did not date anyone else We were boyfriend and girlfriend. My friends were girls and boys. I started dating at age 18 years old The younger children in my family played basketball and baseball on the neighborhood playground 3 Street blocks away from my family home. The kids in my family received trophies for playing baseball For mall park (playground). The kids in my family always got skates for Christmas. I still enjoy and know How to skate 2017 I would go bowling on dates. I loved to bowl at bowling alley (lanes). My first Date was my son father, he was my first boyfriend. He was my first date and I lost my virginity to my son

Father William White.

The first time we made love was in my family home on the couch, In the dining room. I lost my virginity And I got pregnant with my son at age 18. I gave birth to my son at age 19. My mom did not set rules for Me as far as dating. She just did not let me leave the house on a date until I was 18 years of age and she Was very protective. When I was growing up parents were ashamed to sit down and have the birds and the bees talk with Her children. If you were hanging out or with friends your friends and you did not know about the birds And the bees. You learned from friends or other kids or boys, who had experienced the birds and bees Personally. because as I was growing up, I did not have any friends that I actually hang with or socialized With. I was quiet and an introvert that did not do a lot of talking. My older sisters and brothers never Spoke to me about life or the birds and the bees. So when I finally start dating and going out in the World outside my home. I was lost, I did not talk. So, I learned life from experience. In life if you Don't have people who have experienced life to give you the talk about life, The only other teacher On life experience is to experience life on your own accord. That's what I did, I learned everything in Life from experience because prior to dating my son father, All I did on a daily basis is stayed to myself In my family home. The first time I had sex with my son's father, who I lost my virginity to, I got Pregnant. I did not know what I was during. I thought that I was in love because this male was My first everything, my first date, my first sexual experience, my first boyfriend. I was a quiet introvert, That was in the house all day, every day for years only going to school or going out the House to church or going out with my sisters and brothers and my parents. I did not get any talk or Lecture about the birds and the bees from my parents, school, or church. I learn from life personal Experience. I did not have any advice with regards to dating and relationships. With the Opposite sex. The only hobbies I had as a teenage was playing baseball and basketball on the Neighborhood playground or (park) 3 street blocks away from my family home and I watched Television and I loved spending time with my siblings and parents. My mom owned and operated A sweet shop, her sweet shop had a juke box (large record player) or music machine that played Records that is installed in the machine, you just put money in the juke box and press the number Of the record, you want the juke box to play and it played the record. I loved playing the the latest record of the music artists/ singers I liked. I especially loved, the music artists/singer Jerry Butler records and Diana Ross records. So, I would put a quarter in the juke box in my mama Sweet shop and press the number of Diana Ross record or Jerry Butler record and the juke box Machine or Record player would play my selected song. I met my husband when I was standing outside my family 2 story house, He told me hello and kept Walking. I was only 12 years old and a total quiet introvert. I did not have any friends. Other than Going to school and church with my family. I was either inside or sitting or standing outside my family Home that day. I was standing outside my family house. I lived in a neighborhood that most families In the neighborhood, would sit outside their homes, on the porch, the stairs, or on the public side walk In front of their homes. Especially on hot days because we only had fans to cool off in those days 1950s, 1960s and 1970s. I first met my husband when I was age 12 outside my family home. When we met again I had given birth To my son, who was 1 years old. I had already move out my family house. I had already met bobby. Bobby was a married man, who had just separated from his wife and kids. He was still staying in the House that he stayed in when he was still with his wife and kids. We started dating. He would take me by his house after our date. We dated for months. He asked me to move in with him but he was moving out of the house he was staying in. We rented an apartment upstairs over my sister Sylvia, her husband Scott and their children. We stayed together about a year, my son was 2 years old. One day Bobby came home and told me that he was moving out. He gave me no previous warning. I was in shark and in total Disbelief. I was sick with the flu and my son Reginald Age 2 years old was sick with the flu. Everything Belong to him and I did not have a job. The bills were in his name, the apartment was in his name. Everything was in his name. This was my first time living away from my family. He moved all his Furniture out of the apartment. He did not leave any furniture in the apartment. He did not pay Any bills. He gave me no prior warnings. I learned a harsh lesson the first time I moved out my Parents house. My mama would not allow me to move back in the family home. My sister Sylvia Lived directly under my apartment and she would not allow me and my son to stay with her. She had 7 kids plus herself and her husband Scott. But she did not offer us any food or medicine Or a place to stay. I had a sister Mary that lived next door to my mama in the family second 2 story House. That my mama always rented out to tenants. My sister Mary, her husband Allen and their 5 Children rent the upstairs apartment in my family second 2 story house. My mom lived next door In the family home. She would not let me back in the family home. My sister Sylvia live in the Apartment downstairs under my apartment and now I went to my sister Mary, she would not Let me move in with her and her family but she did feed me and my son 2 years old Reginald. And she gave us cold medicine for the flu. My son and I went to my sister Bernadette, she allowed Me and my son to live with her. This is when I met my husband again, Years later. I met him initially When I was 12 years old. I was walking to a neighborhood store. When I ran into him again, His name Was William Lincoln. We started dating but every time we would go out on the date I would Mention Bobby the man that I stayed with. I did not realize my friend all the time was jealous Of my old boyfriend. I was still in love with Bobby. But I stayed with my sister Bernadette and her Family after I stayed with my sister Bernadette for some months. My sister and her husband Separated and she left me and my son Reginald with her husband.

CHAPTER 3

Adulthood

A) Further Education

B) Work and Career

C) Marriage or Formation of Significant Relationships

Her husband asked me to move out this is where William Lincoln, we were dating and he offered to find an apartment for myself, my son and him to live. I moved in with a man I did not know or like that well because I was still in love with bobby, the boyfriend I stayed with for a year. Because I would talk about Bobby every time I went on a date with William Lincoln. The friend I move in with to have a place to stay. Every time I left the apartment to go anywhere when I got back home I got accused of being with Bobby, the Man I stayed with. William Lincoln the man I move in with and stayed with would not only accused me of being with Bobby he would also beat me up. I stayed with this man for at least a year. Having to get beaten up every time I left the house.

A) Marriage or Formation of Significant Relations should have left him but I ended up marrying this abusive Man. I was married to this man for 2 years.

The beatings never stopped. He would beat me and offer to take me to the emergency room. I would call the police but the police could never catch up with him. The one time the police came to the house while my husband was home after he had beaten me up the police did not see any burses on me so the police left and did not do anything with my husband.

He cared about me and he bought me anything I wanted and I did not have to work and he had A good job and we had a car nice things In my rented house. He would shop for groceries. I had Clothes. He loved and adopted my son. My son did not want for anything but when he got angry,

He went temporary insane. His mother and family was jealous of everything he bought for me. I was Forced to sit in the back seat of my family car because my husband mother insisted on sitting in the front seat with my husband. My husband was still attached to his mother's apron String, after we got married. The 2 years my husband and I was married my husband mother force Herself In the front seat of our family car and made me sit in the back seat as the wife.

She made me sit in the back seat of my car as the wife. While she sat in the front seat. Because my husband family had gotten use to my husband buying and doing everything for them. Every time my husband bought anything for me or our home, my husband family would come to my family home with my husband and son and say, we wish we had that. I was an abused wife and I had to put up with jealous, possessive In-laws. My mother-in-law would visit myself, my son and husband and as soon as I open my door, she came into my home and walk in every room of my home to see if my home was clean. My husband began to take my house key I could not get in my own home. He pushed me out on the porch with the Light on and I was in my night gown. If I went with him to his family house if they told him I was rude to them when I got Home that was a beaten and he would offer to take me to the emergency room. My family finally encouraged me to move out. I was young and dumb. I went to Legal Assistance to seek legal counsel (a Lawyer). I got the assistance of a Lawyer. He petition the court to have my Husband leave (to move out) our home. I did not trust to stay in the home that we were renting once He was served with legal papers to move out. So, I stayed with my sister Mary until my husband moved out of our rented home. I went by our home one day after he was served with legal papers to move out He told me that I better leave our home in a threatening manner. I got afraid and I left our home and

Went back to my sister Mary house. Until he left by the court date he was given to move by the court Order. When I went back to the house after my husband moved out he had destroyed my house and Stolen everything out the house. He also stopped payment on the rent. He had already paid for that month rent and the other bills. The utility was turned off. I had to replace rent money because he Stopped payment on the check he paid the rent and other bills with a check payment. He burned all of my clothes, He cut the expensive curtains I had in the living room. He threw red dye on my white living room carpet and white couch. He took an ax to chop the wood tables I had In my living room. He stole all of my appliances out my kitchen and he took my washer and dryer out the garage. He took the televisions. The only thing he did not take was the furniture I had bought before I moved in with him Which were the furniture I had in my den. And bedroom furniture I also bought before he Wrote on the bedroom mirror. "Nothing from Nothing leave Nothing." I cried my eyes out, when I Went back home. After he left my home he moved in with my sister Louise best friend. I suspected that he was cheating on me. I was so Jealous that I would look under bed when I came home from going out the house. Because I did eventually learn to care about him because we live together about a year before we got Married. And he had me spoiled material wise. I got anything I wanted. he would shop for groceries. I did not have to work. He bought all my clothes. But he went temporary insane when he got angry. But to look at him you would never know he was this person.

We lived together about a year, before we got married. We were married for 2 years. When he moved Out of our home by court order. He moved in with my sister Louise best friend. My sister said her friend Told her that she went and bought some new towels for her bathroom. My sister friend told my sister Louise that my husband took my sister friend brand new towel and dried his dog off after he gave the Dog a bath. My sister friend told my sister Louise that she argued with my husband. About using her Brand new towels to dry his dog off. My sister friends told my sister that my husband knocked her out And that she was out for 2 hours. She told my husband he had to leave her apartment. MY sister friend Told my sister my husband took and cut her living room chair up before he left. My husband had problems. He Told me if he could not have me, no one else would have me.

My advice to anyone, I got married when I was 21. I would advise them to wait until you are at least 30 years old before you got married and to get to know the person before you move in or get married. A relationship is important. I dropped out of school when I got pregnant with my son. I got pregnant because I was a quiet introvert. Who was young, and dumb about life. I did not have any friends. My siblings or my parents never Talk to me about life or the birds and bees. So, when I met my son father and we started dating I did not Understand or know anything about sex. I was having sex with my son father because that was what he Wanted to do. That's why I got pregnant the first time we had sex. I gave birth to my son. My son Father did not deserve me. He was never a father to my son. He was too busy partying. He was This type man all his life. He was the type man that got paid on Friday and broke on Saturday From parting his whole pay check away. My mom and family was there for me and my son through The birth of my son and after I gave birth to my son especially my mom. I worked as a waitress for Years after I gave birth to my son. I worked to provide for my son. I met my husband and he adopted My son. My husband name went on my son's birth certificate as the father. My husband paid child Support for my son until he completed high school after we divorced.

My husband and I married in 1972, when my son was age 2. We separate in 1974, after 2 years Of marriage. My son was 4 years old. After my husband and I separated in 1974, I move out of the Rented home we lived in and I moved into an apartment with my son. I received child support from My husband as the adopted father. And I worked part-time as a waitress. When I separated from my husband the only job I was trained in after I gave birth to my son was as a waitress. I decided I was tired of working as a waitress.

B) Further Education

I decided to apply and attend Trident Technical College, Charleston, South Carolina. I attended Trident Technical College in 1975 to 1978. I completed Two different majors. I attended Trident Technical College in 1975 as a Hospital Ward Clerk Major. I completed Hospital Ward Clerk in 1976 after my completion of Hospital Ward Clerk. I was eligible to work in a Hospital as a secretary, and assist the nurses and Doctors. I applied at several Hospital but was unable to find a job as a Hospital Ward Clerk so I returned to Trident Technical College In 1976, in the Major, General Office Secretarial Science. I Completed General Office Secretarial Science in 1978. I applied at Charleston County Hospital and I was Hired In the x-ray department as a secretary. I held this position from 1979 to 1984. After leaving Charleston County Hospital, Charleston, South Carolina.

C) <u>Work and Career</u>

I worked as a clerk in the application office at Charleston City Housing Authority for a year. I also worked for George Sawyer Landscaping Company as a secretary and payroll clerk for a year. I worked in the Secretarial field for 16 years. I return to Trident Technical College in 1987 to 1988. I completed 2 semesters. The last semester I attended Trident Technical College, Charleston, South Carolina I needed to attend classes during the day. If I was going to attend classes during the day. I needed an evening job. I knew the owner of this Grocery store called Jabber. I had never work in the money handling field before, I walked into Jabber Grocery store I asked the owner if he would hire me. he told me if I could watch the cashiers And learn how to operate the cash register, that he would hire me. I went in jabber grocery store one Day I watch the cashiers for about 15 minutes and learned how to operate the cash register and the Owner hired me. I never work in the money handling field before but to my surprise I learn that I Had automatic money handling skills I did not know that until I started working in jabber grocery store As a cashier. I worked for jabber for six months. After six months. I applied at Piggly Wiggly grocery store As a cashier. After working as a cashier for 6 months I was asked by management if I wanted to work in the Front office as a front office teller, cashing checks, selling money orders, accepting SCE&G electric and Gas payment and Southern Bell Telephone company payments. I gave the cashier their money till before they start work, when they went to lunch and return from lunch. I balanced the cashier money till or money drawer at the end of their shift.

I gave the cashier change, Cashed employees checks. And sometime the only teller in the office with a long line of customers to serve. having to close the front office that night and leaving money out for the night manager, before closing the office. I would only Be a penny short. I have excellent money handling skills. I worked for the Charleston Naval Base, Naval Exchange in the money department for a year.

I was assign $25,000 to $30,000 daily and $100,000 on military pay day, to cash military pay checks, employee checks, and to sell money orders. As a cashier in the cash cage, when I was not working on the front window, my job description was to work in the back office and assist in balancing the Naval Exchange money flow. I attend Academy of Hair Design cosmetology college, North Charleston, South Carolina for a year and obtained my cosmetology diploma and license. attended Goose Creek Barber and Styling College, Goose Creek, South Carolina for a year. I obtained my model Diploma. I am also a model. I was trained and work for Maximum Tax Service, North Charleston, South Carolina, for 2 years as A self-employed tax preparer. In 2014 i took and completed a Tax Preparer Course through Jackson Hewitt Tax Service and after completion, I was hired as a part time employee. I Also worked in sales and marketing for 6 years, for a nationwide company, prepaid legal services Inc. I owned and operated my own home base business, I was a self-employed, Independent associate. I recruited membership for the company. The members that I recruited for the Company. Join the company and paid $26.00 a monthly fee, To have 24 hours a day, seven days a week, nationwide access, to prepaid legal service, incorporated attorneys. I worked as a poll manager, for The Board of Voter Registration and Election Commission, Charleston County, South Carolina, from 1986 to 2009. I directed and assisted voters in voting for their political Candidate of choice.

D) Children

My son was my first born. He was born on February 21, 1970. Charleston, South Carolina. I was in labor with my son for 12 hours straight before I gave birth to my son. I was having very heavy labor pains for 12 hours. My daughter was my second born. She was born on November 08, 1983. Charleston, South Carolina. I was in labor with my daughter for 4 hours. I gave birth to my daughter in less hours than I did with my son. I did not exercise when I was pregnant with my son. I have always heard that if your Lazy during your pregnancy, prior to giving birth, the baby will be lazy come out during birth. With My daughter I walked every day up to the day I went into labor to give birth to my daughter. The due date for my daughter was October 23, 1983. My daughter was 2 weeks late. I called the Hospital that was going to deliver my daughter or I was going to give birth to my daughter. And I talk to a doctor. I told the doctor that I refuse to carry my daughter any longer. Because My daughter was two weeks late. The doctor wanted to know who I was. I went to a doctor Appointment at this hospital the day of my daughter's birth because I was two weeks late. The Doctor admitted me. Into the hospital and induce my labor and made me go into labor, While I was in the hospital. So my daughter birth came much sooner than my son's birth of 12 hours Labor. I was in labor only 4 hours with my daughter, even though she was 2 weeks late of her birth due date. My kids have different fathers. My kids are 13 years apart. My son was 13 years old when I had my daughter. He was the only child but I always said I was going to have my daughter by the time I was 30 years old. I had my daughter at age 32. I gave birth to my son when I was 18 years old. My son's birthday is exactly a month before my birthday. My son was born on February 21, 1970, my birthday is March 21, 1951. My son was born when I was still staying in my mom Household. My son was born 6 pound 11 ounces. He was a fat and healthy baby, my mom made sure of that. When my son was 1 year old I moved out my mom house. When my son was 2 years old he loved spaghetti and meatball. I fed my son spaghetti and meatball so much at 2 years old I held the can of spaghetti and meatball up in my son face, I asked him what I had In my hand. He told me that it was spaghetti and meatball. He was just 2 years old. I fed My son spaghetti and meatball so much my brother Gerald would joke about it to my family that my son ate spaghetti and meatball so much he looked like an Italian. When my son was 3 years old he was coming the stairs of my family 2 stories house stair that was on the porch, which extended from upstairs to downstairs. My son lean his body through the Upstairs bannister, he fell through the upstairs bannister on the down stairs porch. I took him To the doctor at the emergency room at the hospital. they did not do any x-ray, they just put His arm in sling. My son had a doctor appointment at the clinic some months later. When I Was taking my son to his doctor's appointment at the clinic. My son was walking behind me I did not see him fall to the ground behind me someone behind me brought it to my attention. That my son had fell to the ground. When I got inside the clinic and the doctor examine my son Reginald he told me my son had a seizure. My son had never had a seizure prior to this day. This doctor is telling me my son just had a seizure. I was in shock. Total disbelief. The doctor ordered tests on my son to find out why he was having seizures. The tests showed that my son was Having mild seizures. Called petite mall seizures. My son would have slight jerking and eyes rolling But it did not last that long. My son was placed on seizure medication. As my son got older The seizures turned into grand mall seizures the jerking and the eye rolling became more serious. But the medication to this day 2017 keeps my son seizures under control. I took a picture of My son as a baby and I took pictures of my son when he was about 9 years old on Easter Sunday. But as my son got older as a teenager, he hated taking pictures. As my son being my only child. He went everywhere with me. My son attended catholic school like I did and all my siblings did. He attended Cathedral Catholic School, Charleston, South Carolina and when he was in 8th grade He attended Sacred Heart Catholic School, Charleston, South Carolina. When my son got in the 8thgrade he got upset with another student and turned a cafeteria table over In the lunch room. I had to take him for counseling before the priest would take him back in the school. My son was 13 years old when I gave birth to my daughter. When I got pregnant before I could tell my son I was pregnant my sister told him I was pregnant. Because he was the only Child for 13 years, when my sister told my son I was pregnant. My son got angry and stormed Out my sister Odessa house. Because my son was the only child for so long, when I was Pregnant I would try to show my son my stomach, he would not look at me my whole pregnancy. He hated that I was pregnant. He also had a problem with my daughter father. When my son became a teenage age 15, his personality changed. I began to seek Adolescence counseling for my son. He would spend a lot of time at my older sister Mary house. My sister Mary would let my son hang out in her den because my son was into sports. He knew Everything about sports. Dallas was his favorite football team. And the Lakers was his basketball Team. My sister told me she allowed my son to hang out in her den and watch sports or television To keep him away from drugs. When my son got in high school and after he left the catholic school And began attending public school, is when I began to have to constantly go to the school because He did not want anyone hitting him. He had to hit back. My son got left back in North Charleston High School, North Charleston, South Carolina. Not because of his academic or his grades being Bad. He got left back in the 9th grade for 4 years strait because he could not stop hitting back. He is very smart to this day 2017. My son don't start fights but he don't want anyone putting their hands on him. My son could not Graduate North Charleston High School, North Charleston, South Carolina because he got kept back In the 9th grade for4 years strait for getting put out of school and missing more than 10 days which Is the maximum days a student is allowed to miss every year. I finally, told the school not to call Anymore, I was not coming to the school. I finally, took my son out public school. North Charleston High School, North Charleston, South Carolina and put him in Job Corps. He got put out Job Corps. He did get his GED from Job Corps, his major course was Auto Body, He did not complete Auto Body. I enrolled my son in Cosmetology College, North Charleston, South Carolina. He graduated Cosmetology College and obtained his Cosmetology Diploma. He met a young lady in Cosmetology College. My son and this young lady just left the Cosmetology College one day and got married Without telling me. His marriage last a year and him and his wife got a divorce. My son attended Trident Technical College and obtained his CNA Certification. I am still hoping he will further his education In the future. My son is a hard worker and he is very intelligent. He is especially good in math, A course I never was good in. I am proud of my son and I love my son and he loves his mom. My son Hated every man friend I ever had over to house. He gave them all the look, that said don't come back Anymore. He did not want his mama to have a man. When he was a teenager and before he finally Got married. My son was trying to block me from having a love life when he was a teenager and before he got married.

My daughter Kimberly Alexis Lincoln Gardner my 2nd child. My son Reginald Lincoln was my only Child for 13 years before I got pregnant with my daughter. I took a long time before I go pregnant With my daughter. I wanted to have a girl because I believed that if you have the boy you should have the girl. But I was determined that I was not going to have my daughter until I turn 30. Or until I found Mr. Right. But I got pregnant for Mr. Rotten. I met my daughter father in a night club. While I was Partying with my best friend and partying partner and some of her female friends. My daughter father Was sitting at the bar in the night club. I went to the bar to get another drink and my daughter father Was sitting at the bar. He spoke to me and I gave him my phone number. It turned out after contacting Him he was in the Navy. He was stationed on the Naval Base, North Charleston, South Carolina. I gave John Moore the man I met at the night club my phone number. He called me, we dated for three Months. I got pregnant, he told me he was married on mother day. He offered me money and he left. He did not tell me he was going to sea for six months. I called this Naval Chaplin I was in contact with On the naval base and he told me that John Moore my daughter's father had left on his ship And that he would be at sea for six months. Before my daughter's father came back from sea. I Had given birth to my daughter. I called the Chaplin on the naval base. I told him that I had given birth To my daughter and could he contact John Moore my daughter's father. When I got out the hospital, My daughter father came by my apartment to see his daughter. When he came in my apartment. My daughter was on the bed screaming to the top of her voice. I had never seen a baby with such a Wide (gate) mouth, my daughter had a big mouth for a baby. My daughter father John Moore and I started dating again after I gave birth to my daughter and he came by my apartment after he came back from sea. He saw his daughter and gave me money for my daughter Kimberly. My daughter father came back to my apartment, He bought his daughter, a crib and he put it together.

He would come by to see me and his daughter. He would try to feed his daughter, my daughter but My daughter as a newborn baby liked eating fast and her father John Moore did not know how to Feed her. He started giving me money on a regular basis for my daughter, his daughter Kimberly. We were also dating again when my daughter started walking at seven months. He came by the house to see her first steps. Sometimes he would come by after she started walking. I would be in the kitchen, he would be in the bedroom. He would hit her and she would come in the kitchen where I was and tell On him. He would just laugh. He wanted me to give my daughter his last name Moore. I said no. When my daughter turned 3 years old I had a problem because I needed more money and my family told me to take John Moore my daughter father to court because he was in the military and my family felt because he was in the military that he might get stationed or transfer to another state and not tell me.

I took him to court I got an attorney through child protective services. He got angry that I took him to Court. He said I started so he was going to finish it. He got an attorney and told the attorney that my Daughter was not his child. He knew she was his child but to spite me he asked for a paternity test My attorney made him pay for the paternity test. He had to pay $300 dollars for the paternity test. We had to meet at a paternity laboratory for the paternity testing. He was their when I got there for The test. He watched his daughter while I went back to take my part of the paternity test. She knew him So, she did not cry. The test came back. 99.9 per cent and up and until the day he died. He always told How my daughter, his daughter paternity test came back 99.9 per cent (positive). We started dating Again, up and until he came by my apartment one day and said his good byes privately to my daughter Kimberly, his 3 years old daughter not saying anything to me that he was being transferred to Jacksonville, Florida with his wife and family. He would still send my daughter Kimberly gifts for Christmas. I was working with my sister Bernadette as her secretary and payroll clerk. She was the Manager, of this. company called George Sawyer Landscaping Company, Charleston, South Carolina. I was in the office alone this day and I pick up the office phone. I decided to call the Pentagon in Washington, DC to see if I could locate my daughter father John Moore. I called the Pentagon Told them I was trying to find out where my daughter father was stationed. I had my daughter father Social Security number because his social security number was on my child support papers and My daughter military ID since he was ordered by Family Court To pay my daughter child support. Before he was transferred out of North Charleston, South Carolina, Naval Base. The Pentagon personnel gave Me his location and how to contact him, I called him, I told him that I told him I would find him. He said he knew I would find him. I would call his mama if I need to contact him. Sometimes during Christmas I would allow my daughter to call her father house his wife was mean.

To my daughter, His wife had cancer. She eventually died from cancer. He would send my daughter clothes. He sent my daughter a dress when she was 9 years old. He told my daughter that his wife bought the dress for my daughter. My daughter said she was going to give the dress to her daughter. When my daughter was 5 years old my daughter and I was out at a sea food restaurant with a friend of mine and my daughter was sitting at the restaurant table and just suddenly, she yelled out real loud "My daddy has a wife." I did not know the child was thinking about her daddy as being married. I did not remember ever telling my daughter her daddy was married. My daughter finally Got a chance to attend her daddy family reunion when she turned 14 years old. My daughter father Wife had already died from cancer. My daughter end up moving to Jacksonville, Florida after she Graduated high school but she sent him an invitation to her graduation the same invitation my Daughter sent to her daddy to come to her high school graduation, he left her high school graduation And took the graduation invitation to child protective services and had her child support turned off. He told her he would not turn her child support off if she attended college. My daughter was So, hurt that she went to legal aid or legal assistance attorney to make her daddy turn her children Support back on but she was not successful. I had my daughter after her high school graduation Attending Trident Technical College, Charleston, South Carolina, her major was legal assistance. I was encouraging my daughter to be an attorney. My daughter and I got into an argument because she wanted a new car on her part time job as a cashier at Wal Mart department Store. I told my daughter she could not afford a new car on a part time job at Wal Mart. We argued I left my house I though She went to her college classes but when I came back home, she was packed and moved out my house. She ran my pressure up sky high. She was diabetic. She became diabetic at age 17 years old. I did not Know where she was. I went to all her school classmates and friends no one knew where she was. I called her best friend from high school and spoke to the best friend and her mama they said they did not know where my daughter was. I am calling the police 2:00 am and 3:00 am I was total stressed out. I finally found out that she was staying with a female older friend. She had met. I called the police and I had the police meet me at this female friend house my daughter was staying with. The police told me My daughter was of age they could not make her come back home. These people made my daughter Take out an order against me to stay away from my daughter. My daughter Kimberly finally moved out the female friends House. And moved in with her best friend from high school parents house. They became like a second Parent to her. I was angry with her best friend parents for taking my daughter in their home. Because Her best friend parents had already told me they would not up hold my daughter in their home but I was glad my daughter was safe with her best friends and her parents. After my daughter moved out my house, she lost her Pell Grant at Trident Technical College as a student. she did not do what was required to keep her Pell Grant in effect. I went to the College with her they told me she had to pay out her pocket to continue attending Trident Technical College that semester. I called her father John Moore in Jacksonville, Florida he had her moved to Jacksonville, Florida with him. My Daughter father and his girlfriend enrolled my daughter in Edward Waters College. Jacksonville, Florida, In the Criminal Justice Major. I had my daughter enrolled in Legal Assistance at Trident Technical College, Charleston, South Carolina. I was trying to encourage my daughter to be a lawyer(attorney). But she lost her Pell Grant Charleston, South Carolina. My daughter met a young man while she attended Edward Waters College, Jacksonville, Florida. They moved in together. They had a son, they both were criminal Justice Majors. they both graduated the same day in the Criminal Justice field. They graduated May 2010. I brought an expensive jewelry box for my daughter graduation with some diamond rings inside the jewelry box.

I made sure one of the diamond ring looked like an engagement ring. My daughter Kimberly Lincoln and her son father Darren Gardner graduated May 2010. They got married August 2010, They both returned to college. They both received their masters in August 2015. My daughter Kimberly received her masters in Mental Health Counseling and her husband Darren received his master in Business Administration. My daughter presently attends college for her doctrine degree. My daughter and her Husband just bought their first home in 2015. Prior to my daughter moving out my house after Receiving her high school diploma. Going back to my daughter's childhood, my daughter did Everything from her childhood to adulthood on time. My daughter Kimberly walked at age 7 months, my daughter's doctor said at age 1 that my daughter needed to be off the bottle because the milk was not good for my daughter gum. I told my daughter one time that she could not have her bottle Anymore and she never cry for her bottle anymore. My daughter Kimberly was potty trained at age 2 years old. Ever since my daughter was old enough, she gave me a card for every holiday. If my daughter Kimberly did not have any money she made the card for me. My dream for my daughter ever since she was 10 years old was for my daughter to become a model. I paid for her to go to modeling school. She had a couple of photo shoot to make up her model representation card and she had a verbal agreement with the model school she was attending but this modeling school never found her any jobs. So, every time a model scout came through Charleston, South Carolina where my daughter and I lived. I would take my daughter to the hotel where they held The model scout meeting. The host would pick the kids they felt had modeling potential. My daughter got picked. The model audition was held out of state. At a hotel. My daughter and other contestants walked the runway in front of model agents at the foot of the runway to be chosen by the model agent The model audition my daughter and i went to was in Atlanta, Georgia, my daughter was number 350 She walked the runway hoping to be picked. She was not picked. I spent all that money for her to Compete and she was not chosen. My daughter attended another model scout meeting. Held at a hotel in Charleston, South Carolina. My daughter got picked. The model audition was held out Of state in Boston, Massachusetts at a hotel, my daughter was number 725 contestant. She went Through the same process. she went through in Atlanta, Georgia. My daughter was number 725 she walked the runaway hoping to be picked. She was not picked or chosen by the model agent at the foot of the Runway. I spent more money pursuing my dream of my daughter becoming a model. And she still Was not chosen or picked as a model. My daughter and i left the model convention held in Boston, Massachuetts after not being chosen as a model for the second time. My daughter was disappointed flying back on the airplane to Atlanta, Georgia and to Charleston, South Carolina. When my daughter Kimberly and I returned home to Charleston, South Carolina, my daughter received a brochure to compete in Miss Teen State Pageant for Charleston, South Carolina. I had to raise $2,000 dollar for my daughter to compete in the State Pageant, the State Pageant was held in Greenville, South Carolina.

My daughter competed in the Pageant Optional Contest as well as the Queen Pageant. My daughter competed in the Spokes Model Contest (she wrote and enter her speech in order to be a participate in the Spokes Model Optional Contest and she submitted a photo of herself to compete in the best photo optional contest. For the Spokes Model Optional Contest, my daughter Kimberly wrote and submitted a speech on "what Friendship Means to Me." There were three contestants that participated in the Optional spokes Model Contest of The South Carolina State Teen Pageant my daughter Kimberly Lincoln a black teen contestant, a second black girl teen contestant and a white girl teen contestant. they all wrote a speech in order to participate in the Spokes Model Contest of the South Carolina State Teen Pageant Optional Contest. The second black teen girl contestant also, wrote her speech on the same subject my daughter wrote her speech on which was "what Friendship Means to Me." The white teen girl contestant wrote her speech on a different subject than my daughter Kimberly Lincoln a (black) teen contestant and the second black teen girl contestant. The contestants that participate in the South Carolina State Teen Pageant Optional Contest. They wrote their speech they submit their speech to the Pageant office prior to the day Of the Pageant. On the day of the South Carolina State Teen Pageant Optional Contest the contestant practice before the contest. Once the contest begins the contestants get in line behind the runway and walk the runway individually in order to say their speech. My daughter Kimberly Lincoln was the First to walk the runway to the podium to say her speech like she practiced earlier. She got to the Podium with full confidence, her speech was on "what Friendship Means to Me" She did an excellent job and she left the podium waking back off the runway. As her mother I thought she should have won the Spokes Model Contest. The other contestant, the second black teen girl contestant was next to said her speech on "What Friendship Means to Me" She walk the runway to the podium. She said her speech, she was confident She did a good job but she was already attending college to become a brain surgeon and she had already taken a course in public speaking. The third and last contestant a white teen girl contestant, she wrote her Speech on a different subject. She walked the runway to the podium, she was tripping over her words when she said her speech after she said her speech she walked off the runway. The Optional Contest was the same day as the

South Carolina Teen Queen Pageant but it was held that night. The Optional Contest was early that day. So, after the Optional Contest early that day the contestants already knew that night of South Carolina state Teen Queen Pageant and award ceremony the contestants who won early that day in the Optional Contest, they were told who won 1st, 2nd or 3rd place in the Optional Contest and they knew that night what award they were going to receive that night at the awards ceremony where all the contestants were given there awards for participation in The South Carolina State Teen Queen Pageant and Optional Contest. My daughter participated in the Queen Pageant that night but she was not a finalist. There were other Optional Contests the contestant were allow to participate in but there was a cost of $50:00 for each Optional contest you sign up for. I signed my daughter up for 2 Optional Contest the Spokes Model Contest and The Best Photo Contest. I paid $50.00 for each. My daughter also submitted her Photo for the best Photo Contest she did not win or got an award for her submission. Some of the other Optional Contest was Modeling, Acting. Singing. The night of the South Carolina State Teen Queen Pageant my daughter was one of the contestants but she was not a finalist contestant. The second black teen girl that Participated in Spokes Model Contest with my daughter Kimberly who won the contest for her speech "What Friendship Means to Me." she also won The South Carolina State Teen Pageant Queen Title and She along with my daughter and the other young white teen girl contestant won the entitlement to participation in the South Carolina State National Teen Pageant representing the State of South Carolina against other contestants on a National level. The night of the South Carolina State Teen Queen Pageant my daughter Participated as a contest she was not a finalist or won the Queen title, she had the opportunity to compete with the young lady that did win the Queen title of South Carolina State Teen Pageant, she was a contestant in the South Carolina State Teen Queen Pageant and Optional Contest received awards for her participation and she won 1st place for her speech "What Friendship Means To Me "The awards for The South Carolina State Teen Queen Pageant and The Optional Contest were given out the night of the Pageant after completion of the Pageant in which a South Carolina State Teen Pageant Queen was chosen. The award ceremony personnel gave out awards after the Pageant Queen was chosen. My daughter Kimberly received trophies and plaque for her participation in both The Queen Pageant and Optional Spokes Model Contest. When my daughter trophies and plaque were given out I was so excited that I did not pay attention to what was actually on the trophies and plaque until I got back in my home in Charleston, South Carolina and I looked at the print of the trophies and plaque and I saw 2nd place instead of 1st place. When I realize the mistake I called the South Carolina State Teen Pageant and Brought it to their attention. They acknowledge that there was a mistake made. I waited for them to get back in contact with me. They never did so I called them a week later and the personnel I Spoke to told me there was not a mistake. I kept trying to get to the right person so I could get My daughter the award she won. But as the weeks goes on I kept being told that there was no mistake After initially being told there was an error made. The day of the Optional Contests, after the contest the contestants were told what award they won and which one they should be expecting to receive That night of the Queen Pageant and during the award ceremony. I just made the dumb Mistake of not look at the print on the trophies and plaque before I left the Pageant and award Ceremony. That night before I left to go back home the next day to Charleston, South Carolina. Which is when I realize the error. I spoke to a friend about it he was a prominent Pastor. He told me just leave it alone if I want my daughter to have a good experience with the Pageant personnel. Instead I kept pursuing the matter. My thoughts were my daughter worked hard on her speech and she was told she won 1st place for her speech. My daughter and I was out in the hot sun raising the $2,000 dollars she needed to participated in the Pageant. We traveled on the Greyhound bus the distance from Charleston, South Carolina to Greenville, South Carolina with her pageant Gown in my hands the whole trip. Along with all the other inconvenience. I kept calling and I was eventually told that if I kept pursuing the matter that when my daughter participated in South Carolina National Pageant to represent the State of South Carolina on a National level at Walt Disney World at the Hilton Hotel, during the Thanksgiving Holiday that my daughter would not be treated accordingly as the other contestants. I kept pursuing and When my daughter and I got to Walt Disney World at the Hilton Hotel there was no reception as a Pageant contestant. She participated and received a large Trophy with the other contestants. But other than that there were very little reception and acknowledgement. She did not have any contact with the other contestants and very little contact with the Pageant personnel. She did not get to spend time in Walt Disney World with the Other contestants or take pictures. After my daughter got her trophy we got the balance of my money that I had already paid for the hotel and my daughter Kimberly I left the Hilton Hotel, Walt Disney World Orlando, Florida and return to our home town of the city of Charleston, South Carolina. I did not allow her to participate as a contestant in the South Carolina National Teen Queen Pageant that night other than the large trophy she participated to received. They never contacted me and I never call them again that was the end of my daughter Kimberly participation in Pageants to become a model. I invested more money to accomplish my dream for my daughter Kimberly To become a model. My daughter did participate 8:00 am that morning for her speech. "What Friendship Means to Me." The Contestants Dress attire was a white suit I bought a white suit on my belts department store credit card for her to Say her speech at the National Pageant in Walt Disney World at the Hilton Hotel but I was running Late to catch the train in Charleston, South Carolina I did not get to the train station on time enough to have my luggage at the train station when I arrived so my daughter speech was 8:00 am that morning and My luggage did not get to the train station Orlando, Florida until 12:00 noon I did not have a car or the extra money to get another white suit for my daughter so my daughter said her speech in a jump suit that I had Bought for her she did not win for her speech at National Pageant.

Finally, my daughter Kimberly last year in high school at Garrett Academy, North Charleston, South Carolina. I took her to Holiday Inn Hotel in Mt Pleasant, South Carolina to a Model Agency Hosting.

That was looking for 90 models 45 models the first day and 45 models the second day. My daughter Kimberly was picked the first day of hosting to pick 90 total models. My daughter Kimberly paid out her Pocket as a cashier at Walmart $900 dollars for her model photo shoot and model representation card And she signed her model contract with the model agency as a professional model but the model agency Did not find any jobs for my daughter Kimberly, as the mother of my daughter Kimberly

I eventually began promoting my daughter Kimberly model career on a website I setup on the internet in which I paid a monthly fee. She was finally picked as a model After I spent thousands of dollars in my attempt to pursue my dream for my daughter Kimberly to Become a professional model. I had spent thousands of dollars in my pursuant of my daughter becoming a Professional model with a major model agency. I was determined to have my daughter become a model After, spending thousands of dollars paying for her to attend modeling school, model conventions in Atlanta, George, model convention in Boston Massachuettes, paying for my daughter Kimberly to attend and participate in South Carolina State Teen Pageant and South Carolina National Teen Pageant. I spent thousands of dollars in my attempt to have my daughter Kimberly become and obtain a modeling contract with a major modeling agency from age 10 to age 18 years old. I invested thousands of dollars pursuing my dream to have my daughter Kimberly become a model with a major model agency traveling to Atlanta, George and Boston, Massachuette to model convention hoping she would be picked by a major model agency. I paid for her to attend modeling school in the family home town of Charleston, South Carolina and invested in my daughter Kimberly participating in South Carolina State Teen Pageant Held in Greenville, South Carolina and South Carolina National Teen Pageant held in Orlando, Florida Walt Disney World at the Hilton Hotel. After all my investments (paying for clothes, travel, hotels, etc.) My daughter Kimberly finally became a model with a major model agency in the family home state and neighboring city of Mt. Pleasant, South Carolina. My investments in my daughter was not bad investments because even Thought my daughter was not chosen, through her participation in the model conventions, modeling school And State and National Teen pageants, her participation kept her involved in a positive environment and around other positive kids, who knew what they wanted out of life and that they wanted to pursue a successful educational future.

My daughter Kimberly wanted to work at age 14 years old but as soon as she turned 15 she started working at Walmart department store in Mt Pleasant, South Carolina. My daughter Kimberly graduate high school in 2002 From Garrett Academy High School. After graduation she moved to Jacksonville, Florida to live with her Father John Moore a retired Naval

Chief in the United States Navy. She transferred her cashier position At Mt. Pleasant, South Carolina Walmart to Jacksonville, Florida Walmart. She worked at Walmart Jacksonville, Florida around attending Edwards Water College, Jacksonville, Florida as a Criminal Justice Major student. She worked at Walmart until she graduated Edwards Waters college in May 2010. After she graduated she started working for AT&T Cellular company for 5 years. My daughter Kimberly Has been working since age 15 years old. She married and still works to this day. She is now married to Her college sweet heart Darren Gardner with two kids a son Jalen 8 years old and a daughter Morgan Age 3 years old. The relationship between my son Reginald Lincoln and my daughter Kimberly Lincoln Gardner (married) was one of an older brother and baby sister. Because my son was age 13 years old When I got pregnant with my daughter Kimberly, when my son first heard from my baby sister Odessa That I was pregnant and going to have another baby he was angry because he was the only child for 13 Years. My son was always jealous of my daughter to a certain extent but he always played the big Brother role with his baby sister, he was very protective. She cried for him to take her with him when He left the house. He would take her on the playground with him. Before I gave birth to my daughter,

My son was my only child I took him everywhere with me. When he was not with me he was with my Family. My son had seizures since he was 3 years old. So my son was a sickly child. My son most of His young life and adult life he would have seizures and I would have to call EMS whenever he had A seizure, especially when he became old enough to take his medication on his own. My son would not tell me when he ran out of his seizure medicine. I would have to call EMS to take him To the Hospital. When he got in eight grade at Sacred Heart Catholic School, Charleston, South Carolina he turned the lunch table over on other students. The priest told me that he would not Take him back in school until I took him for adolescent counseling. The priest paid for the counseling When my son left Sacred Heart Catholic School, Charleston, South Carolina and I enrolled him in North Charleston High School he was diagnosed with emotional handicap I feel he was diagnosed with emotional handicap because of him having been exposed to my husband beating me up in front of him for 3 years. That is why I feel anyone in an abusive relationship with kids should leave the relationship if only for the kids mental, emotional, physical and verbal health and safety because there is all different types of abuse. I feel the abuse that my son was exposed to from my abusive Relationship with my husband in front of my son for 3 years affected my son emotionally I was Young but if I had it to do over again I would not allow my son to be exposed to that mental, Emotional, physical, and verbal abuse. My son being the only child for 13 years he was with me Everywhere I went except work. And when he was not with me he was with my family. When my Son was about 4 or 5 years old my son and I was walking from my apartment to my sister Mary House about 8 street blocks from my apartment to my sister's house my son was tired walking So my son and I was at the traffic light a street block away from my sister Mary house waiting For the light to change my son Reginald just yelled out to this man in his car, he said, hey Man give us a ride. or a lift. When my daughter Kimberly was borned it was like having a baby for the first time because my son Was 13 years old and it was a long time since I had a baby. The least little thing went wrong with My daughter I would take her to the Franklin C Fetter Clinic, Charleston, South Carolina. The nurses At the clinic was tired seeing me. They knew I was a new mom and that I had not had a child in 13 years. They knew me as soon as I walked in the clinic door. It was like Ms. Lincoln what is wrong now. When my son got in his teens and started hang with his cousins his age and got interested in sports since age 15 years old he would mostly hang out at my sister Mary house in her den in front of her television set. My sister was like his second mama and my sister husband was like a father to my son Reginald. Plus when my son became a teenager is when I began to have problem with him. I first Started having problems when my son Reginald was in the 8th grade at Sacred Heart Catholic School Charleston, South Carolina and pushed the school lunch table over on the other students. That's when I started having problem with my son Reginald. After the priest refused to take him back in Sacred Heart Catholic School pending me taking my son Reginald to a psychologist for adolescent counseling. After this incident my son began to be my problem child. But my son had seizures since he was 3 years Old. And he watched my husband abuse and beat me in front of him for 3 years, actually beat me with Him in my arms at age 3 years old. I placed my son in North Charleston High

School, North Charleston, South Carolina. That boy got put out of school every year for four years in the 9th grade. He never made It out of 9th grade because he fought in school every year and the school suspended him every year More than ten days which mean he could not get promoted if he missed more than 10 days per school Year he was smart. But they knew he was diagnosed as emotional handicap and they still put him out School every year for 4 years more than ten days. They knew he would not be eligible to be promoted. My son and I argued because he wanted to do things his way and made his head hard. But he was Intelligent especially in math. I took him out North Charleston High School, North Charleston, South Carolina because he was kept in 9th grade 4 years straight and would not be able to graduate High School. But when I took him out Hight School and put him in Job Corps he graduated and received His GED in 6 months and received his driving License. He did not complete his auto body major in Job Corps. I enrolled him in Cosmetology College, North Charleston, South Carolina To get him out my sister Mary house in front of the television set and to help him get a trade and I Encourage him to get his CNA Certification but he never used either major. Maybe he will attend college In the future in a major of his choice. My daughter Kimberly were just the opposite of my son they had different fathers. They each has there Own personalities. My son had difficulties growing up with his seizures since he was 3 years old and he Witnessed my husband abusing me has also affected my son over his years. But my son Reginald is honest, he is hard working, he is intelligent and he loves his mama and his sister. He is very protective Of his mama and his sister. My daughter Kimberly relationship with my son was close. My daughter Kimberly and my son Reginald was my shadow when they were growing up. I kept my daughter and my Son close to me when they were young and growing up. If you saw me you saw my daughter when she Was young and when my son were young if you saw me you saw my son. I kept a tighter hold on my Daughter Kimberly because she was a girl. I was a strict mother with my daughter than I did my son. My daughter Kimberly were not allowed to go anywhere unless I took her. My dream for my daughter Was for her to be a model. I pursued that dream with my daughter her teen years. I was strict with my Daughter Kimberly I did not allow my daughter to go anywhere without me I took her and her friendsWhere ever they wanted to go. She wanted to work I worked with her and helped her find her First job at 15 years old. I took her to work and I picked her up from work. My daughter Kimberly Started working at Walmart part-time after school. My daughter Kimberly spoiled me rotten with her part-Time job at Walmart. Every special occasion came up my daughter use her pay check from Walmart To acknowledge the special occasion. Every Mother's Day my daughter Kimberly took me to Ryan's Restaurant to eat. Every Birthday my daughter Kimberly took me out to Ryan's Restaurant to eat. Every other special occasion came up if my daughter Kimberly did not take me out to eat I got at least Flowers and a card. If my daughter Kimberly and I shopped at payless shoe store and they had a buy one Pair of shoes get one pair half off. My daughter was not leaving out that store unless she bought me a Pair of shoes too. My daughter Kimberly attended a trade school Garrett Academy High School in 9th grade. She met Her high school sweet heart Rod. She wanted me to meet him I told her I was not going to meet him. She was determined I was going to meet him. I always took her everywhere she went, she did not go Anywhere without me taking her. I was strict I was determined she was not going to follow her cousins Getting pregnant. So I was really strict with my daughter Kimberly. I was determined my daughter Kimberly was going to at least finished high school without getting pregnant. I was looking out for her because I wanted her to finish high school and go to college. But I was also looking out for myself because if she Got pregnant at a young age that would be like me having another baby because I had to help her raise the baby and she may have had to drop out of school like I did when I got pregnant with my Son in high school. So I did not want to encourage a relationship with this boy she wanted me to meet. She was just in 9th grade. She was determined I was going to me him. One Sunday my daughter Kimberly told me that she wanted to go to the movies with her friend. I told her she was not going Anywhere without me taking her. She told me I always want to take her everywhere she go. I told Her the only way she was going to the movies is if I took her. I took her and her friend Candy to the Movies. When we got to the movies, I got a bag of popcorn and sat at the front of the movie theatre. My daughter Kimberly and her friend Candy went back out of the movie where I was. I thought they Were gone to get popcorn and was going to return to watch the movie. My daughter and her friend Candy never returned to the movie with me. After the movie was over I left out the movie I was Watching to look for my daughter and her friend Candy. When I got in the movie theatre lobby my Daughter Kimberly and her friend Candy was in the movie theatre lobby with two boys her friend Candy grab one of the boys and said he was her boyfriend and the other boy I ask him his name. He told Me his name was Rod. I recognized his name as the boy my daughter wanted me to meet. I took my Daughter Kimberly to the car. I was very angry. My daughter Kimberly kept saying no mama he was Saying I know your mama did not let you out here with this short dress on. This boy was saying yes Mam no mam and at the same time sneaking out of school with my daughter Kimberly to have sex With my daughter. They would skip class. I allowed my daughter Kimberly boyfriend Rod to come To my apartment. They left and went to the store. I was outside sitting in my boyfriend work truck In my drive way when they returned from the store. They went inside my apartment while I was In my drive way with my boyfriend. Before my boyfriend left he joked and told me my daughter And her boyfriend might have been having sex. And He jokingly told me to take my time opening My front door. When I walked in my apartment my daughter and her boyfriend Rod was standing In front of the stove in my living room hugging. I asked them jokingly what they were doing my Daughter boyfriend Rod said no mam I would not disrespect your house like that. He was yes mam, no mam Me at the same time sweating my daughter Kimberly. My daughter Kimberly always knew how to maneuver to make situations work for herself. In school She knew how to get along with her teachers to make sure she got the grade she needed. When she worked at Walmart in her teen years while she was attending high school she got so many Certificates from Walmart department store as a cashier. The managers loved my daughter. My daughter Kimberly was trained to work all the different department in Walmart department Store. The managers could pull my daughter Kimberly from the front end of the store as a cashier to work customer service, layaway, jewelry, every department in Walmart department store in Mt Pleasant, South Carolina. My daughter Kimberly transferred to Walmart in Jacksonville, Florida When she attended Edwards College. Jacksonville, Florida. She left Walmart after she graduated In Jacksonville, Florida. She started working for AT&T Cellular making $50,000 dollars a year going From store to store. She left AT&T Cellular. She started working as a Probation Officer after she Graduated from Edwards College, Jacksonville, Florida in the Criminal Justice Major. She left her Job as Probation Officer when she started working as a Social Worker for DCF Department of Children and Family. She just got her Master In Mental Health Counseling. She wants to open Her own business as a mental Health Counselor after she receives her Doctrine Degree as a Mental Health Counselor in which she is presently attending College for her Mental Health Counseling Doctrine. Degree. My daughter was in Middle school she was on the NAACP Youth Group team. I was an Executive on the NAACP Board at the same time. My dream for my daughter was to become a model when she was age 10 through 18 my daughter went To Model conventions in Atlanta, Georgia and Boston, Massachusetts hoping she would get picked as a Contestant by model agents at the convention. My daughter Kimberly and I would walk around the lake and Hampton park in Charleston, South Carolina, in order to keep the weight off. My daughter and I also Went to the Gym. I attended my daughter modeling classes with her and I attended my daughter model Shoot with her when she was picked as a model and had to have a photo shoot in order to have her Model representation card made up. My daughter and I played tennis also to keep the weight off. My daughter also participated in South Carolina State Teen pageant in Greenville, South Carolina And her South Carolina National Teen Pageant held at the Walt Disney World Hilton Hotel Orlando, Florida. I took my daughter and her friends to the skating ring and also to Chuckee Cheese a restaurant For kids, with rides and pizza. I took my kids to the County Fair. My son Reginald and daughter Kimberly attended Church Every Sunday. We went grocery shopping. My Kids and I hang out at my mama house together with Family members. My kids and I attended family Birthday parties. My daughter Kimberly and I was a member of NAACP as members together. My daughter Kimberly was a member of the Youth program and I was on the NAACP Executive Board. My son Reginald and I watch sports together. My son Reginald is a big sports fan. Dallas Cowboys is his football team and the Los Angeles Lakers is his Basketball team. My son Reginald and daughter Kimberly went to eat at various restaurants on Special occasions.

The family Traditions I try to establish is attending church (catholic mass) every Sunday as Catholics. I have a tradition of preparing the same meal since my kids were young every Thanksgiving, Christmas I prepare a Turkey, macaroni and cheese, collard greens, and rice, Sweet potato pie, potato salad, cranberry sauce and egg nog. On New Years Day I cook the traditional hopping jones and rice a tradition handed down from my mama and family since I was a young girl. Going to the County Fair is another tradition passed down from when my mama took me and my sister and brothers since I was a young girl. My kids also bought me a Christmas Gift and a Birthday Gift or card On Mother's Day. The tradition calling on Holidays wishing Good will whatever the Holiday is. Merry Christmas, Happy Easter, Happy New Year, Happy Birthday. The tradition to buy an outfit for Easter and attend church on Easter Sunday. The tradition to buy an outfit for Christmas. The sentimental value I have is the pictures of myself and my kids as they grew up, my kids High School Diploma, my daughter Kimberly and my son Reginald baby pictures. My daughter Kimberly Degree from college, my son Reginald Diploma from Cosmetology College, My son Reginald GED from Job Corps. My daughter Kimberly model representation card. My modeling representation card. My grandkids and pictures of my grandkids. My High School Diploma, my college certification, and family picture of me and my Children, A family picture or photo. They will be passed down to my Kids should something happen to me their mother. My kids are the love of my life from the day they were born. I have always wanted children. I gave birth to my son at the age of 18 years of age. If I had it to do again I would have waited before I had my son. I would have graduated from high school first. I gave birth to my daughter later in life when I was 32 years Of age, If I had it to do over I would make better choices in who I fathered my children by. My son father was the type man that gets paid on Friday and broke on Saturday. My son is his only children and he has never been a father to my son to this day. I got married when my son was 2 years of age. My husband adopted my son after I got married. My son father signed adoption papers. Relieving himself of all rights to my son Reginald his only child. After my husband and I got a divorced he chose to stop being a father to my son Reginald his adopted child. But his name was on my son birth certificate after he adopted my son Reginald. He still was responsible as my son adopted father after we divorced. My son Reginald natural father William white fathered my son in blood only but today my son Reginald Still loves his natural born father even though he was never a father to him his whole life to this day. My daughter Kimberly father John Moore deserted me when I told him I was 3 months pregnant. He went to sea for six months as a naval chief in the Unites States Navy. He did not tell me he was Going to sea. I was in contact with a Chaplin on the same Naval Base my daughter father John Moore Was station on in North Charleston, South Carolina. I was able to call the Chaplin when I gave birth and the Naval Chaplin contacted my daughter's father and told my daughter father that I had given birth to my daughter Kimberly. When my daughter father John Moore returned from being at sea for six Months he came by to see my daughter Kimberly, his daughter at my apartment in Charleston, South Carolina where we lived. He gave me $100 dollars and we started dating again. He was in my daughter Kimberly life from the day of her birth. I took him to court. For child support. That was the smartest thing I ever did when it came to my daughter's father. Because the Navy transferred or stationed him in Jacksonville, Florida my daughter's father John Moore came by my apartment pick my 3 years old Daughter up and said his personal good byes. He never mentioned to me that he was being transferred or stationed in Jacksonville, Florida before he left Charleston, South Carolina. But I took him to court Before he was transferred to Jacksonville, Florida so I had his social security number. I called the Pentagon in Washington, DC gave the Pentagon my daughter's father name John Moore and social Security number and the Pentagon personnel told me where my daughter's father John Moore was Located in Jacksonville, Florida. I found my daughter Kimberly father. I called him and told him I found Him, he said he knew I would find him. He was married he lived with his wife but I was able to keep in Contact with him through his mother in Miami, Florida. But I raised my kids by myself without my kidsFathers and my satisfaction of raising my kids were my love for my kids and as my kids only responsible Parent. I chose to bring my kids in this world knowing I would be totally responsible for my kids without Their father's assistance. My love for my kids as a mother kept me going to be the best single mother I can to my children. My son Reginald needed me because he started having seizures since he was three years old.

I struggled with my son medically since he was 3 years. But I was blessed that the medicine my Son Reginald was prescribed for his seizures kept his seizures under control. It was difficult for me as a mother watching my son (my child) have seizures all these year and constantly having to call EMS for emergencies from my son Reginald having unexpected seizures most of the time. Because my son as he got older was not as responsible in taking his medicine and I should have left my husband sooner than I did and not aloud my husband to abuse me for so long in front of my son Reginald from 2 years of age to 4 years of age. I feel my son being diagnosed as emotionally handicap in high school I feel I may be partially responsible for not leaving my husband sooner. I learned a lesson. That it is not good for Children to be exposed to parental abusive relationship But I was young when I was married to my husband and I am glad my family finally encouraged me to leave my abusive, sick, disturbed husband. It was difficult raising my kids especially, during times when i was not working and my children needed Clothes, shoes, or Gift for Christmas. Every year my kids needed Gift for Christmas. Many Christmas I had to find a male friend to be Santa Clauses for my children. There were plenty days I did not know how I was going to pay the rent or put food on the table or pay the electricity bill or phone bill. There were many days I had to get on my knees as a Religious Catholic and pray to God to help me Provide for my kids and my household. I feel my mama was my example. She raised 14 kids as a single Parents after daddy died. I Always tried to instill the family Catholic Religious Faith and value in my children. Everyone in my family, the Mitchell family was baptized into the Catholic Faith immediately after birth. And I have always tried to carry on and Instill the traditional Mitchell family value in my children starting with their immediate baptism after their birth. My Parents were middle class Catholic. My parents baptized all the children in the family all 16 Children, the family 8 boys and 8 girls. As catholic all of the grands, great grands, and great, great, grands children were baptized into the catholic faith

As a baby it is a family tradition that my parents John Mitchell and Christabell Mitchell started. I always instilled in my children, my son Reginald and my daughter Kimberly to never take or steal what does not belong to them. My model is I won't take anything from you and you don't take anything from me I had my children baptized as babies and we attended church every Sunday.

When my daughter was about 6 years old. I would take her grocery shopping with me to Piggly Wiggly grocery store In my neighborhood. An soon as I walk In the grocery store my daughter Kimberly would disappear into the cookie aisle. One day I was shopping in the Piggly Wiggly Grocery store as soon as I walk in the store my daughter Kimberly disappeared in the cookie Aisle when I looked for my 6 years old daughter in the store security guard approached me with My daughter Kimberly he knew me and management knew me and my daughter, we shopped Piggly Wiggly as a regular customer we lived around the corner from piggly wiggly. The security Guard approach me with my 6 years old daughter that he caught eating a pack of chocolate Chip cookies. Apparently my 6 years old daughter liked chocolate chip cookies I did not know she Liked it that much because I received food stamps I bought the chocolate chip cookie when I bought groceries I was so embarrassed because I shopped this grocery store every day I was a regular customer and I was always strict on my kids about stealing. To this day my kids knew not to steal I did not tolerated and instill this value in my children. She hates when I tell that story about her to this day so I don't tell the story but it was embarrassing to me it was funny at the same time.

Because she was just 6 years old I bought the chocolate chip cookie all the time I just did not know She liked it that much. If she had made it known to me I would have bought it for her on a regular Basis. I began to buy chocolate cookies regularly because I did not won't the incident happening Again. He turned her over to me when I got home my daughter Kimberly got a whipping an a talking Too. I never had that problem again. At age 6 years old she got the message. To this day she knows I don't tolerate stealing. My daughter Kimberly never stole again to this day that I know of. I was to Embarrassed to go back inside Piggly Wiggly grocery store again. I knew the manager that made it A little easier. I instilled education in my kids. I always told my kids to always have your own because when you have to Depend on other people you have to go through changes or kiss people's behind. I also told my kids Sometimes you have to swallow your pride when you are in need. And have to ask for help or Assistance. I always tried to instill in my children not to be around the wrong people who don't Want anything out of life because you are the product of the environment In which you surround Yourself and you are the product of the company you keep. I always tried to keep my daughter Kimberly Around kids that wanted something out of life and in a positive environment with positive people. My dream for my daughter Kimberly from age 10 was to become a professional model. from age 10 year old my daughter Kimberly had a career in modeling instilled in her. She attended modeling school at age 10 years old she had a model shoot through the model school she attended at age 10 years of age After her Model shoot with this modeling school she was offered a verbal model contract with this Modeling School she attended in Charleston, South Carolina after her model shoot with this modeling School. The School never found her any jobs as a model because the model school booking agent that My daughter Kimberly had the verbal model contract moved out of state. The booking agent had my daughter Kimberly Model Photo shoot conducted at her apartment in historic down town Charleston, South Carolina this female booking agent with the modeling school my daughter attended at age 10. The booking agent left the modeling school and got a job with a movie production company. My daughter Kimberly verbal agreement with this modeling school she attended was never Honored by the modeling school manager after the booking agent that was going to promote My daughter Kimberly left to work at the movie production company. My daughter was Acknowledge by this modeling school as one of their model and my daughter representation Modeling card was place inside the modeling school as one of their model but the manager Never found my daughter any jobs. And honored her verbal agreement she had with the Booking agent that left the modeling school that promise to promote my daughter Kimberly. At age 10 years of age my daughter missed out on her verbal agreement with the modeling School she attended but I never gave up on my dream as her mother for her to become a Professional model. I kept my daughter Kimberly from age 10 in modeling. She participated in South Carolina State and National Teen Pageants. I tried to put my daughter Kimberly in good schools. My daughter Kimberly Attend the Military Magnet Middle School and Garrett Academy trade High School, North Charleston, South

Carolina. And also Sacred Heart Catholic School (pre-school), Charleston, South Carolina. My Daughter Kimberly attended Mitchell Elementary School, Charleston, South Carolina. The first year my daughter Kimberly left Mitchell Elementary School, Charleston, South Carolina to Attend Rivers Middle School. My daughter Kimberly had this smart mouth teacher at Mitchell Elementary School in Charleston, South Carolina. All of my daughter Kimberly teachers at Mitchell Elementary School, Charleston, South Carolina thought I was a parent that took up for my elementary School daughter. I was protective of my daughter Kimberly and she was spoiled. I don't think I was as bad as her teachers at Mitchell Elementary portray me to be. So, my daughter Kimberly last year at Mitchell Elementary School Charleston, South Carolina. my daughter Kimberly smart mouth teacher Told my daughter Kimberly that your mama protected you at Mitchell Elementary School But I bet She won't be able to protect you when you attend River Middle School. That teacher knew what she Was talking about and I dreaded my daughter Kimberly going to Rivers Middle School Charleston, South Carolina every day because we live in the same neighborhood and Rivers Middle had students Fighting every day outside the school. I did not want my daughter Kimberly to attend Rivers Middle School. But the kids that lived in the neighborhood was stuck with going to Rivers Middle School. Unless the parents could afford to pay for their children to go to a private Catholic School. I could not Afford to put my daughter Kimberly back in Catholic School. My daughter Kimberly attended (private School) Sacred heart Catholic School Charleston, South Carolina in pre-school at age 5 years old. But I could not afford to pay for my Daughter Kimberly to attend Sacred Heart Catholic School again. I was stuck putting my young child In Rivers Middle School. My daughter Kimberly was just getting out of Elementary School. Into a rough Middle School that fought every day and the kids in the school gang you. Its more than one person fighting you at the same time you could not win because you were out number. And the other students is in a circle around you while you are getting ganged. The first year I enrolled my scary young protected daughter Kimberly all her life she was a model Attended modeling school, attended model conventions. She was around kids who were interested in Being a model. She was not use to being in a violent environment. I kept her with me, she was not

Allowed to go anywhere without me. I was stuck with enrolling my daughter in Rivers Middle School Charleston, South Carolina. The school of gangs, where students got ganged every day. A school Where the school found a gun In a student locker the same year I enrolled my child that just Graduated from elementary school. I enrolled my daughter in Rivers Middle School I hated taking My child to Rivers every day against my better judgement. Every day I pick my child up from Rivers Middle School my daughter Kimberly was asking me about or talking about something she Was never exposed. Every day I picked my daughter Kimberly up from Rivers Middle School, Charleston, South Carolina my young daughter that just graduated elementary school, her first year in Middle School. Every day I picked her up my young innocent daughter is talking about horrible things she was Never exposed to her who life. Terrible things that I intentionally did not discuss with her when I Talked to my daughter about the" birds and the bees" and the facts of life. When I picked up my daughter Kimberly from Rivers Middle School, Charleston, South Carolina my Daughter Kimberly told me that one of the student at Rivers Middle School told other students At Rivers Middle School that she sucked his dick. My daughter Kimberly was just 12 years old. And she just got out of elementary school. My young elementary graduate daughter was not exposed to This kind of language in elementary school. This was the first time my daughter Kimberly ever heard These words spoken directly in reference to her. I did not discuss this subject with my daughter when I talked and read the birds and bees to my daughter 10-12 years old daughter when we discussed the Birds and Bees, this was abuse. These kids at this school was being abused emotionally, mentally, Physical, and verbally. When this male student that made this abusive statement about my daughter I Went to his grandma house and reported him. When I saw him again he acted very embarrassed This was a bad school. But the students in the neighborhood was stuck attending this school because They lived in the neighborhood and the students had to attend this school in their neighborhood. Every day I picked my daughter up from this terrible school I was not surprised what came out my Daughter Kimberly mouth. But when my daughter teacher at Mitchell Elementary School told my Daughter Kimberly that her mother would not be able to protect her once she attended Rivers Middle School she knew what she was talking about. I did not want my daughter at this horrible school but I was between a rock and a hard place and my daughter was suffering the consequences on a daily Basis. I told everyone that if you wanted your kids to learn about the facts of life enrolled your Kids in Rivers Middle School, Charleston, South Carolina. I finally got the opportunity to transfer my 12 Year old daughter out this terrible abusive school. My daughter Kimberly was traumatized she Probably still have bad dreams about that terrible school to this day But I had no choice but to enroll My daughter in Rivers Middle School, Charleston, South Carolina because we lived in the neighborhood. The parents need to sue the school district over this horrible school now that I think about having to Enroll my innocent child in this school But I finally got the opportunity to transfer my child to another School. I finally got the opportunity to transfer my daughter Kimberly out of Rivers Middle School. Charleston, South Carolina. I picked my daughter Kimberly up from school she told me that This girl wanted to fight her. I told her she should have reported this student to the principal. I told her When I pick her up the next morning to take her to her dental appointment at 10:30 am that I would report this student to the principal. When I dropped my daughter Kimberly off at Rivers Middle School that next morning before my daughter Kimberly got out the car, she said mama by the time you pick me back up at 10:30 am for my dental appointment this girl will have already fought me. I did not listen to my daughter Kimberly. When I got back to Rivers Middle School that morning at 10:30 am to pick my daughter Kimberly up for her 10:30 am dental appointment. This girl along with Her other 5 gang members had followed my daughter Kimberly around all morning to fight her, they Went into my daughter Kimberly third period science class that morning. The girl that wanted to fight My daughter and her other 5 female student gang members. The female student gang member that was Already In my daughter Kimberly third period science class with her attacked my daughter Kimberly first. After the female student gang member in my daughter Kimberly science class attack my daughter Kimberly then the female student that threatened to fight my daughter Kimberly and the other 4 female student gang members came in my daughter Kimberly third period science class at the Same time and attack her while she was in her science class with her male science teacher along with Her science classmates. Those 6 female student gang members came in my daughter Kimberly third period science class and attack my daughter Kimberly but other students that was not involved initially was attacking my 12 years old daughter. There was a total of 10 kids on my 12 years old child. my 12 years old daughter just graduate elementary school. This was my daughter first year in Middle School. I sheltered my daughter all her life. She was not allowed to go anywhere without me her Whole short life. but I could not protect my daughter from this attack. My daughter had just graduated From Mitchell Elementary School prior to enrolling in Rivers Middle School. My daughter Kimberly teacher At Mitchell Elementary School told my daughter that her mama would not be able to protect her once She Attended Rivers Middle School. My daughter teacher at Mitchell Elementary School statement came true for my daughter and that teacher knew what she was Talking about.

It was raining the day those kids ganged my daughter Kimberly. The kids ganged my daughter was hitting my 12 year old daughter Kimberly with umbrellas, they were kicking my daughter, boxing my daughter. I could have had a dead child that day; when I got to the school to pick my daughter Kimberly up for her 10:30am dental appointment that morning. I enter Rivers Middle School to find out that my daughter was in the principal office and the principal was calling all the gang members in his office.

After the principal got the student involved in his office he called me in his office and told me what had Happen. I was so angry I referred to all the students gang members that was in the principal office with my daughter, as little bob cats. One of the student told me she was not a bob cat. The principal suspended these female student gang members. He also suspended my daughter Kimberly. He stated that my daughter was not so innocent. When I initially walked into in the principal office to pick my daughter up for her dental appointment that morning. I saw River Middle School Charleston, South Carolina assigned city police officer standing at the school principal front office counter and I heard the principal telling the school city of Charleston, South Carolina police officer that he could leave. This was before I found out what was going on with my daughter Kimberly. I was in the principal office with the Rivers Middle School assigned City of Charleston, South Caroline police Officer, my child had just got ganged and this City of Charleston, South Carolina school assigned police officer said Nothing to me. He did not even acknowledge me. My understanding later is that the school principal should have called for police assistance and he did not call for police assistance. After I took my daughter out of the principal office and my daughter was also suspended along with her fellow students that ganged her and could have killed her. I went to find my daughter homeroom teacher to get my daughter Kimberly homework while, she was on suspension. My daughter homeroom teacher was in the library. When I went into the school library to ask my daughter Kimberly homeroom teacher for my daughter Kimberly homework while she was on suspension. Two students that was in my daughter class and in the library with my daughter homeroom teacher started fighting. My daughter teacher sat down she did not try to part or stop these two students in her class that she took to the library from fighting. I had to stop the students from fighting. I feel this teacher was either afraid or tired of getting hit by these students fights. Rivers Middle School was a school of gangs the students got ganged on a daily basis. I could understand why the school personnel found a gun in a student Locker that year. Because the fights was not one on one fights, these students actually got ganged on a daily basis. If I had to go to school to get an education but had to worry about getting beaten up every day I attend school it is unimaginable. My daughter Kimberly began to fail a couple of her school classes. The parents were allowed to sit in their kids class room if their child was failing. I was not working so I would go on a daily basis to sit in my daughter Kimberly classes that she was failing to help her improve her grades. I was walking in my daughter Kimberly school hallway one day, while I was sitting In my daughter Kimberly classes to help her improve on her grades and I saw one of my daughter Kimberly friend and classmate standing in the school hallway by the school principal office, I asked her why she Was standing in the hallway she looked afraid, she told me that someone had taken her $5.00 but she was standing by the principal office but afraid to go into the principal office to report her missing $5.00. The Students at Rivers Middle School was terrified of going to the principal office to report an incident. Terrified of being ganged. When I attempted to go to my daughter homeroom class to get her homework. I was told by one of my daughter teacher what happened to my daughter Kimberly. He made reference to what happened to my daughter and stated that he had never seen anything like it before.

He also said that it took 10 teachers to keep a total of 10 kids of my Daughter Kimberly. I went to speak to my daughter science teacher Mr. Herd, who class my daughter was in when the incident occurred. I saw him he complained that his shoulder was hurting. I just kept imagining him hopefully holding my daughter and protecting her from all the attacks against her I am just glad she was in a male teacher class when theses student entered my daughter Kimberly science class and attacked her. Before i took my daughter home from school that day after she got ganged. I had one of my daughter teacher told me that it took 10 teachers to keep these kids off my daughter. He said he had never seen anything like it before. I had Rivers Middle School students attacking my 12 years old daughter with umbrellas, kinking her, boxing her, her teacher Mr. Herd was complaining about his shoulder hurting.

Before I left the school. I think my daughter was lucky her teacher that day was a male teacher I never Asked him but I felt he probably protected her. There was to many students on my one 12 years old Daughter. I could have had a dead child that day. When I got home that day my child had a mark under Her eye. Her dad was in the U S military (Navy) I took my daughter to the Naval Hospital, North Charleston, South Carolina. about two days after my daughter was ganged in Rivers Middle School by these students. I went to the School district. I was historically upset that my child was ganged by all these students and that I could Have had a dead child. I went down to school district I asked for my daughter to be transferred to another School. The school district agree that I can have my daughter Kimberly transferred to a different school. About a couple days after the fight the school principal sent his School police officer (City of Charleston, South Carolina police officer) to my house he told me that if I charge the students that ganged my daughter (traumatized) my 12 years old daughter. The Charleston, South Carolina City assigned police officer state that He would charge my daughter also. That made me angry, I could have had a dead child if those 10 teachers Had not kept those 10 students of my 12 years old daughter. My child probably still has flash backs from the trauma of the attacks against her by these 10 Rivers Middle School students and that Charleston, South Carolina

City assigned police officer came to my house telling me he would have my child, (daughter Kimberly) charged. After that principal already suspended my daughter for being ganged by his Students and after he did not do his job by getting the Charleston city police involve and he jeopardized my child (daughter Kimberly) life because if those 10 teachers did not get involved I probably would have had a dead child (daughter) that day because that was too many people on one person especially a 12 years old child. I asked that police officer to please leave my house. After asking that police officer to leave my home I was satisfied, I was not going to let these Rivers Middle School female student gang members get away with what they did to my child Kimberly. I went over the Rivers Middle School police officer head; I went to his Charleston, South Carolina City police department supervisor. This Rivers Middle School Charleston City assigned police officer female supervisor called a meeting with everyone involved. She (Rivers Middle School city assigned police officer supervisor) held a meeting in the school library with students that ganged my daughter, the science teacher, who class my daughter was in when these students attacked my daughter, my daughter and the police supervisor conducting the meeting.

The Charleston City of Charleston police Supervisor allowed everyone to tell their story as to what happened. Each student that ganged my daughter stated that they just happened to be passing my daughter science class that my daughter was in when they came in the class to attack my daughter. My daughter science teacher stated what happen., because he was in the classroom when the student came in his class to attack my daughter. The female Charleston City police office supervisor conducting the meeting after everyone stated what happened. She told the student female gang members that they attacked my daughter. She stated, she told them that she was going to have them taken to the Charleston, South Carolina City police department. She stated, she told them that she was going to have them charged and turned over to family court for prosecution. When the court day came up I did not attend but these student was charged. I can't remember the charge when your attacked by more than one person. These Rivers Middle School female student gang members Were going to my daughter classmate and friends at Rivers Middle School house to fight them. My Daughter's friend parents got involved. After being charged and process this Rivers Middle School Female student gang member that threatened my daughter initially was in my neighborhood one day. My daughter was outside my apartment with her friend, they were standing by my car. My daughter and her friend went into my daughter Kimberly bedroom. This Rivers Middle School female Student gang member that initiated the school gang attack against my daughter was now in my neighborhood threatening my daughter and her friend outside my apartment. After my daughter and Her friend went into my daughter's room. This Rivers Middle School female student gang member took An egg and threw it on the outside of my apartment building and outside my daughter bedroom window. I called the Charleston City police department on this young Rivers Middle School female student gang member and My daughter Kimberly Rivers Middle School fellow schoolmate just process through the Charleston City Police department and referred to Family Court to be processed for ganging my daughter at Rivers Middle School is now outside my home (my apartment) harassing my daughter and her friend. I just called the Police and she across the street on the neighborhood playground refusing to leave the neighborhood; Knowing I just called the police on her. This young girl is on the neighborhood playground across from my apartment and home laughing say the police is not coming, the police is not coming. This was a Horrible evil little girl. I was glad I had her processed for ganging my daughter. Otherwise she would not Have left my daughter alone. I did not have my daughter transferred to another school until the next school term because the school year was almost over at that school.)

My daughter will always remember middle school Because I took my daughter out Rivers Middle School That next school (term) year and I transferred my daughter to Courtney Middle School. This school was a Little better than Rives Middle School. This school was not a school of gangs. This school was about 14 streets blocks Away from Rivers Middle School in the same neighborhood. This school Courtney Middle School also had fights among the students. But by this time I think my daughter had decided She was going to fight back after being ganged. My daughter was not use to being around Violence until she attended Rivers Middle School. My daughter was my shadow if you saw me you saw My daughter.

I did not let my daughter go anywhere unless I took her I was a strict mother but My daughter still had to deal with being beaten up at Courtney Middle School. The only different between Rivers Middle School and Courtney Middle was the students at Courtney Middle School did not gang you the fights was one on one fights and the principal suspended the Students and the students were not allowed back to school without their parents. When the students Returned to school with their parents in that way the students and the parents sat down with the Principal before they were allowed to return to school. In this way the principal got the parents involved. But one day this big tall female student decided to fight my daughter Kimberly. My daughter fought back She took her book bag and fought this girl back. This girl was bigger and taller than my daughter but I Guess my daughter had decided she was going to fight back plus this time she was not being ganged By ten students all at once. The next school my daughter attended was the Military Magnet Middle School, North Charleston, South Carolina. This was my daughter first year in a mix school with the exception, of preschool at Sacred Heart Catholic School, Charleston, South Carolina. With the exception of pre=school all the school my daughter Kimberly attended was all black students. She attended Mitchell Elementary School, Rivers Middle School, And Courtney Middle School, all black school in the neighborhood we lived. This particular day My daughter as a member of a mix school (with different races); Military Magnet Middle School, North Charleston, South Carolina; the first year at a new public military School 90% percent black students and 10% Percent white student with a lot of controversy going on in the school. My daughter will always remember Middle School.

My daughter next school was Garrett Academy High School a trade school mix school She finally attended a school with no problems. Because the Garrett Academy High School Principal was a female and she did not tolerate students that was not disciplined in her School. She would suspend her student in a heart beat. Students at the Garrett Academy High School either shape up or ship out. Garrett Academy High School, North Charleston, South Caroline where my Daughter attended had a no-nonsense Principal and I was finally Happy to have my daughter Kimberly attend a school where I could Finally have a piece of mind for her and myself as her mother.

My daughter Kimberly graduate Garrett Academy High School in the Trade of Marketing. She attended her Senior Prom with a perfect Gentlemen. His name was Phillip. He picked my daughter Kimberly up at her door with a corsage. My daughter Kimberly and her date Phillip looked like movie Stars with their sun glasses sitting in the back of that Limousine rented by her Perfect Gentlemen prom date as they attend their senior prom. My daughter Kimberly wore a $300 dollar satin gown and sash around her Shoulder and her perfect gentlemen date Phillip wore a Black suit and tie Looking very sexy.

I discipline my kids by talking to them and I did use a belt. My mama use the electric Cord to discipline myself and sister and brothers and if we try to get away from my Mama when she was disciplining myself and my sisters and brothers my mama would Throw the first thing she got her hands on. Myself and my siblings would try to get away from my mama as fast as we could before she got her hands on something to throw at myself and my sisters and brothers. But I don't discipline my grandchildren. I don't like my daughter or her husband disciplining my grandchildren. I spoil my granddaughter 3 years old Morgan and my grandson 8 years old Jalen. Today I believe in talking to Children I heard on television and I presently believe that whipping your child affects Children mentally, emotionally, their self-esteem and self-worth it has a negative Effect on children growth and it is the decision maker as far as children growing up To be productive human being and productive adults in life. Today I believe in talking to children. Today I think it is abusive to discipline your Children the old fashion way when I grew up and when I raised my children. Today I feel whipping your child lands parent in jail and the children taken away from them.

E) <u>Ongoing interests and Hobbies</u>

My interests are as a professional model who have only invested in modeling but still has not made any money in modeling as of the year 2017. My interest is to have an updated Model Photo shoot and have an updated model representative card made and pursue jobs in the modeling field for my age range and to return college to further my career and to have my book I just wrote on my family history publish and spending time with my son, daughter and grandchildren.

My hobbies are watching television, writing my recent family history book, exercising, Reading and Playing tennis,

CHAPTER 4

Overview

What has provided me the greatest satisfaction in life has been giving birth and raisingMy children Reginald Lincoln and Kimberly Lincoln Gardner. Being an excellent mother,Household provider, to encourage positivity professionalism and educational values in my children. To instill in my children to always pursue their dreams in life and to live as productive and responsible adult, to pursue my dreams in life. Educationally and professionally. To buy my own home and live comfortably. To have grandchildren and spoil them rotten. My daughter Kimberly has graduate high school from Garrett High School North Charleston, South Carolina. She moved to Jacksonville, Florida Where her father lived. My daughter Kimberly father John Moore enrolled her in Edwards Waters College, Jacksonville, Florida. She has obtained her Criminal Justice Degree From Edwards Waters College, Jacksonville, Florida where she met and married her Husband Darren Gardner, who has also obtained his Criminal Justice Degree. My daughter Kimberly and her husband Darren has children 3 years old Morgan and 8 years old Jalen. My daughter Kimberly and her husband Darren has bought a family home And automobile. Both my daughter Kimberly and her husband Darren has Return to college and obtain their Master Degree. My Daughter obtained her Master Degree in Mental Health counseling and her husband Darren has obtained His Master Degree in Business Administration. My daughter and her husband has Recently invested in real estate. My daughter Kimberly is presently attending college To obtain her Doctrine Degree in Mental Health Counseling.

My son Reginald Lincoln attended Cosmetology College. He has his Cosmetology Diploma. My son Reginald Lincoln obtained his GED Diploma and Driver License From Job Corps. He also has his CNA Diploma from Trident Technical College, North Charleston, South Carolina. My son Reginald Lincoln got married after Graduating Cosmetology College. He is a hard worker. My son Reginald Lincoln Also, recently obtained his own car. My son Reginald Lincoln is a hard worker And a very responsible adult.

My daughter also participated in South Carolina State and National Teen Pageant. My daughter Kimberly is also a Professional Model. I am also a professional model. I have also obtained my Model Diploma. I attended Trident Technical College, Charleston, South Carolina I attended under 2 major Courses: General Office Secretary and Hospital Ward Clerk (working in a hospital As a secretary) assisting the nurses and doctors. I attended Academy of Hair Design, North Charleston, South Carolina I obtained my Cosmetology Diploma and License. I also attended Goose Creek Barber and Styling College, Goose Creek, South Carolina. I am a Certified Tax Preparer through Internal Revenue Service to Prepare Income Taxes.

I sometimes find myself thinking back about when I was young and growing up in the 1950s and 1960s in the city of Charleston, South Carolina Eastside. how the world has Changed. I was a young girl, the third youngest of 16 children born to Christabell and John Mitchell. I have often heard of the 1950s and 60s referred to as the golden age in America. because of the Stability of the families, rising income, wholesome TV shows and low crime rates. I miss and wish we had more of these golden days when my families and families in this era, ate dinner together every evening, the children was well manner and disciplined, they said yes mam and no man to their elder, and neighbors said hello to each other.

When I was young and growing up the Eastside of the City of Charleston, South Carolina During the 1950s and 60s my parents Christabell and John Mitchell placed all 16 of the Children in the family in a line and the family walked to the neighborhood church Our lady of Mercy Catholic Church streets blocks away from the family home. Now the family still attends Our Lady of Mercy Catholic Church but the children and Family members (descendent) of Christabell and John Mitchell drives their automobiles To church (catholic mass) every Sunday. I remember when I was young and growing up on the City of Charleston, South Carolina Eastside. The Families in my neighborhood sat outside their homes on the sidewalks outside of their homes. I remember walking down the streets of my neighborhood and noticing the elder female of the family wearing just a bra and bottom with no top. I remember how the families in the neighborhood would leave their windows up and doors open anytime of the day or night. I remember how the neighborhood families would sit on ther porch any time of the day and night just to enjoy the cool air and breeze.

Families back in the 1950s and 60s use whatever means possible to keep cool from The Hot summer heat because the only mean of keeping cool was the use of an electric Fan or the cool air and breeze. The families in the neighborhood bought their electric fans from neighborhood department stores. The electric fans were placed in the windows and on the floors to accommodate family members from the summer heat. Air conditioning unit had not been invented yet in the 1950s and 60s. But families of today 2017 use air condition units to stay cool.

When i was young and growing up on the Eastside of the City of Charleston, South Carolina in the 1950s and 1960s the children of the families in the neighborhood was Able to play and walk the streets in the neighborhood with supervision and neighbors Kept an eye on the children in the neighborhood but the neighborhood was safe. Now if a child walk or wonder the neighborhood streets unsupervised he or she May end up on a milk carton with the caption MISSING placed above. Today if a child Walk of wonder the streets unsupervised he or she May end up molested and Possibly killed. When I was young and growing up in the 1950s and 1960s parents whip their Children with belts and electric cord. Today if a parent whip their children With a belt and electric cord the parent may be jailed and the child or children Is taken away from the parent or parents. When I was young and growing up in the 1950s and 60s on the Eastside of the City of Charleston, South Carolina if parents left their children in the hot Automobile during hot summer heat they were not taken to the police station and locked up or jailed and have their children taken away from them. but now where I live in Jacksonville Florida, in 2017 parent are taken to the police station locked up or jail and have their children taken away from them if they leave their children in their car unattended or unsupervised Especially in the hot summer heat. In the 1950s and 1960s when I was young and growing up the children in My neighborhood felt free to get dirty or play in the mud and if we drop the food We were eating on the ground we picked it up and kiss it to the lord and ate it. Now you would have to wash your hands down with all these sanitizers. When I was young and growing up in the 1950s and 1960s the siblings in my family As teenager and young adults had a good time watching a movie or playing games and Going out to the movies and going to a night clubs. Now going to the movie or out to a night Club is not as safe with all the crime of night club and movie theatre shooting. In the 1950s and 1960s when I was young growing up we had 3 to 4 channels that had Wholesome family shows. Now in 2017 we have the internet and cable with thousands Of channels. In the 1950s and 1960s when I was young and growing up most families had a mom And dad at home. Now 2017 it is just 1 mom or 1 dad in some homes. As children in my neighborhood on the Eastside of the City of Charleston, South Carolina As the third child of 16 children. My mama and older sibling always watched the younger Children. My mama would take the younger children to the county fair. To the movies. In the 1950s and 60s families in my neighborhood also had neighbors that kept an eye On children in the neighborhood and neighbors were also allow to discipline the children in the neighborhood. As a child in the 1950s and 60s we were not allowed to wonder the Neighborhood unattended or unsupervised. But as a teenager and a young adult our Parents gave us a lead way to travel outside out neighborhood but we felt safe. We had crime in the 50s and 60s but just less violent. There was neighborhood fights Mostly fighting with your fist hardly anyone shooting each other. Today 2017 everyone have a gun. If you fight someone off the muscle or with Your fist now days they will most likely shoot you if they have a gun on them or leave To get a gun to shoot you. In the 50s and 60s 70s when I was young and growing up on the Eastside of the City of Charleston, South Carolina. I remember paying 10 cents and 15 cents for public Transportation the city bus. Now the fare is $1.50 cents. In 1950s and 60s when I was young and growing up families had corded telephones Now everyone have cell phone and I phones. In 1950s and 60s when I was young and growing up, if you missed a show on TV There was a possibility you would never see it again. Today if you miss a show on TV You will possibly have dozens of chances to see it, including the possibility of buying It on something called a DVD or you can record it. In the 1950s when I was young growing up. There was no internet, no text messaging, No I phones of any kind of computers, no emails no instant messaging. People had to communicate with each other the old fashion way. Talking to each other in person, face to face. In the 50s the country was racially segregated In the 50s when I was young and growing up. Woman had very limited choices for a Career or had to be a stay at home mom. Now 2017 we have women in charge of companies, secretary of state of the United of America, some Are judges, Presidential Nominee, doctors, nurses etc. In 1950s and 60s when I was young growing up We did not have a black President. In 2008 to 2016 we had the first black President of the United states of America, President Barack Obama. In 50s and 60s minorities were heavily discriminated against. Now they are Receiving more and more rights. In the 50s and 60s when I was young growing up. If I wanted to see my friends I would go Outside in my neighborhood where I grew up on the Eastside of the City of Charleston, South Carolina and hang out with them out in the streets outside my home. Now Socializing seems to be mostly done via Facebook and text messaging. In the 1950s and 1960s when I was young growing up on the Eastside of the City of Charleston, South Carolina if I could not see my friends in person I would call them up so there was some contact but Now that has been replaced with communicating on a screen. Now you have to worry about every little detail about yourself being mentioned all over the web. Even if you don't use Facebook or twitter yourself people can still mention what you talk about between friends and things about you online

Historically Significant Events the family members lived through Montgomery Bus Boycott

Rosa Parks and the Montgomery Bus Boycott on December 1, 1955. Rosa Parks refused To give up her seat on a bus in Montgomery Alabama and sparked the American civil rights movement of the 20th century. The Montgomery Bus Boycott, in which African Americans refused to ride the city buses in Montgomery, Alabama to protest segregation Seating took place from December 1955 to December 29 1956 and is regarded as the First large scale demonstration against segregation in the United States on December 1, 1955, for days before the boycott began. Rosa Parks an African American woman Refuse to yield her seat to a white man on a Montgomery bus she was arrested and fined. The boycott of the public by blacks in Montgomery began on the day of Paris court Hearings and at lasted 381 days. The United States Supreme Court ultimately ordered Montgomery to integrate its bus system.

Rosa Parks and the Montgomery Bus Boycott:

Rosa Parks refuses to yield her bus seat and one of the leaders of the boycott a young pastor name Martin Luther King Jr. (1929-1968) emerged as a prominent National Leader of the American Civil Rights Movement the wake of the action.

1) Montgomery bus Boycott: Rosa Parkas refuses to yield her bus seat

2) Montgomery bus Boycott: African American Mobilized

3) Montgomery Bus Boycott: Integration at last

4) Boycott puts Martin Luther King Jr in the Spotlight

Rosa Parks was the first African American woman to refuse to give up her seat.

School segregation

School segregation and Equal Education Opportunity. In Brown vs. Brown of Education 34 US 483 (1954) The Supreme Court out lawed segregated public Education facilities for Blacks and whites at the state level. The Civil Rights Act of 1954 Ended all state and local Laws requiring segregation. Racial segregation in the United States as a general term, Includes the segregation or Hyper-segregation of facilities, services and opportunities Such as housing, medical care, education, employment and transportation, along racial Lines. The expression most often refers to the legally or socially enforces separation of African Americans from other races but also applies to the general discrimination against People of color by white communities. The term refers to the physical separation and Provision of so call separate but equal facilities.

43rd President—George W Bush left the country in a depression. 44th President Barrack Obama—became the president of the United States of America During depression—1st Black President 2008-2016 1st Woman President Nominee—2016 Hilary Clinton 45th President of the United States of America-Donald Trump 2017 no political background Hurricane Hugo—1989 disastrous hurricane Police Shooting against young black male 2015-2016 Police Officers kills Statewide 2015-2016 911—Terrorists Attacks in New York City Airport Terrorists Attack at Ft. Lauderdale Florida 2016

The start of the Great Depression October 29, 1929, my mother and father were Born and lived during this period in time. On this day, the stock market crashed and Was renamed "DarkTuesday" many people were left jobless and even homeless after Only a few years. The end of the great depression came about in 1941 with Americas entry into world War 2. Americas sided with Britain, France and the Soviet Union against Germany, Italy and Japan. The loss of lives in the war was staggering. The European part of the war ended with Germany surrender in May 1995. Japan surrender in September 1945, after the US dropped Atomic bombs on Hiroshima and Nagasaki.

I did not have anyone close to me serve in World War 2 But my parents Christabell and John Mitchell were around during the Great Depression and World War 2. I do not have any memory or experience of the Great Depression or World War 2 but I have read about it and my mom and dad lived through this period. The end of the Great Depression came about in 1941 with Americas entry into World War 2. After the US dropped atomic bombs on Hiroshima and Nagasaki. October 29, 1929 was a dark day in history "Black Tuesday" is the day that the Stock market crash, officially setting off the Great Depression. Unemployment Sky rocketed a quarter of the work force was without jobs by 1933 and many People became homeless. President Herbert Hoover attempted to handle the Crisis but he was unable to improve the situation. In 1932 Franklin Delano Roosevelt was elected President and he promise "A New Day" for the American People. Congress created the Work Progress Administration(WPA) which Offered work relief for Thousands of people. The End to Great Depression Came about in 1941 with America's entry into World War 2 The loss of lives in the War was staggering after the US dropped the Atomic bombs on Hiroshima and Nagasaki.

The Vietnam War

The Jungle War 1965-1968

January 20, 1965—Lyndon B. Johnson takes the oath as President of the United States of America and declares we can never again stand aside pridefully in isolation, horrific Dangers and troubles that we once called foreign, now lives among us.

Domestic protests against American participation in the Vietnam War have been <u>Vietnam War </u>credited with shortening the war by both anti-war protesters themselves and by Supporters of the war effort, who felt that fears of a domestic backlash forced both President Lyndon B Johnson and Richard Nixon to limit United States involvements in the conflict. However, this view of the ant-i war movements influence and impact arguably been significantly over stated. Army bases, such as Fort Hood where three soldiers were imprisoned in 1966 for Refusing to serve in Vietnam. In April 1967, the Civil Rights leader Martin Luther King Added his voice to the protests arguing that the "Madness of Vietnam" need to cease Immediately, unilateral United States withdrawal.

Events in the America Rights Movement

Martin Luther King Jr first arrest in Montgomery, 1955

Significance:

Constitutional Amendment forbids any State from depriving citizens of their rights and privileges and defines citizenship. Supreme Courts rules that separate but equal facilities for different races is legal Gives legal approval to Jim Crow Laws Creation of NAACP 1909 NAACP successfully challenges state laws that restricted black Voting registration February 19, 2014.

Black History Milestones

The African American people struggle for freedom was then and remains today. Explore black   history milestone and events that shaped African American history, Including the civil war, abolition of slavery and civil rights movements.

Slavery comes to North America 1619

To satisfy the labor needs of the rapidly growing north American colonies, white European settlers turned in the early 17ᵗʰ century from indentured servants (mostly poorer indentured servants (mostly poorer Europeans) to a cheaper, more plentiful labor source, African slaves, beginning around 1619, when dutch ships brought 20 Africans ashore at the British colony of James town. Slavery spread quickly through the American colonies. Though it is impossible to give accurate figures, some historians have Estimated that 6 to 7 million slaves were imported to the new world during the 18ᵗʰ Century after depriving the American continents of its most valuable resources its healthiest and ablest men and woman.

African American

Struggles one key in the fight for progress

Dr. Martin Luther King Jr. was so eloquent when he spoke of the Arc of Humanity, that It is long but it bends towards justice. I don't think this was blind optimism based on A political understating and knowledge of the history of struggle for freedom that has Made great advances over the centuries base on that understanding. Dr. King believed The people would ultimately win our party shares in that belief. Frederick Douglas viewed That without struggles there is no progress, suggest that with struggle there is progress.

The history of the African American people is a history of struggles. That is how we got here and that is how we will win as a group, with struggle there is progress.

It took the civil war (still the bloodiest war in our history) to end slavery and establish the United States of America. That is how important the black question was Jim Crow. 1830 the term came to mean the American system of racial segregation Embodied in the Jim Crow. The African American people struggle for freedom was then and remains today Central in the fight for democracy and progress. From the struggles against slavery To today's struggle against structural racism and for democracy for all the African American people continues to play a strategic role in the fight for progress. Because United States racism and capitalism are solely linked. The fight against racism and For equality has always also had great revolutionary potential. That centrality of the struggle of the African American people is rooted in a culture` Of struggle and resistance.

I think there is something special about every decade. There was a positive Aspects as well as negative But looking back, It is all about the memories and I have great Memories.

The in their car unsupervised they safe and was not Jail or their children was not taken away from them. Now if parents leave Their children unattended or unsupervised the may be taken to jail and locked Up and their children is taken away from them+ found out what was going on with my daughter of Charleston, South Carolina in her early teens to move in and live with my brother William, his wife and kids. She returned home after she graduated high school My baby sister Odessa also left home to go live with my brother William but when she got off the bus As a young girl and mother, She was kidnapped by this man and was force to live a life of drugs and a lady of the street and was not Allow to come back home to the family until she was older in age. She had a daughter for this man But he would not allow her to bring the child with her when he finally allow her to come back home t The family. My sister came back home. I was very happy to have her back home again. My sister came Back home she went for substance abuse she got off the drugs. She met someone who loved he They had two kids together a son and a daughter. She had two kids before she left Charleston, South Carolina the family home town to live with my brother William and his wife and kids. When she was kidnapped by this man against her Will as a young girl when she got off the bus in New York. My Mother raised her daughter and son she had before left home to live with my brother William. loll s s s

Printed in the United States
By Bookmasters